FASHION

Inside the Fashion Business

The "mystery" of fashion changes has fascinated not only economists and sociologists, social historians and cultural anthropologists, but also philosophers and moralists, poets, playwrights, and novelists.
(Gregory, 1947)

Ilaria Caielli
She has two degrees, one in Art History and Criticism and one in Fashion Communication and Culture. An expert and great fashion enthusiast, she collaborates with various publications including *Il Corriere della Sera* and *Vanity Fair Italia*. She manages the editorial content for major Made in Italy fashion brands. For the past ten years, she has lived abroad in China, the United Arab Emirates, the Seychelles Islands and Cyprus. She is the author of the book, *UAE 101: Stories and Cultural Learning,* for which she won the Future Stars Awards, Arabian Business Awards and Online Shopping Awards. Short guide to buying on the internet.

BEYOND

FASHION

Inside the Fashion Business

ILARIA CAIELLI

 HOAKI

Hoaki Books, S.L.
C/ Ausiàs March, 128
08013 Barcelona, Spain
T. 0034 935 952 283
F. 0034 932 654 883
info@hoaki.com
www.hoaki.com

hoaki_books

Beyond Fashion
Inside the Fashion Business

ISBN: 978-84-17656-73-7

Original title: *Fashionland. La Moda oltre l'Abito*

Author: Ilaria Caielli
Translation: Emma Sayers
Editing: Martina Panarello - Maristella Olivotto
Layout: Wendy Moreira
Cover design: Claudia Martínez Alonso
Front cover image: Jacob Lund/Shutterstock.com

D.L.: B 1071-2022
Printed in Turkey

CONTENTS

INTRODUCTION

Once upon a time there was a tailor's boutique, one's Sunday best, a provincial tailor's workshop, a pattern shop and a fabric shop. There was a time when daughters wanted to look like their mothers: mature, elegant and sophisticated, a time when there were no credit cards and the fashion business was operated by just a few agencies. Then came the years of freedom of expression: skirts got shorter, mothers wanted to look like their daughters, *prêt-à-porter*, globalisation, low-cost delocalised manufacturing, fast-fashion, e-commerce and social media.

Like all creative expressions, fashion (a bit like art) has the ability to reflect the evolution of history, to capture and translate the aspirations of a society into its own specific language. Branded for decades as the most frivolous of disciplines, in today's society of images its growing influence in our lives and in the world economy cannot be ignored.

Fashion, as it is understood today, came into being in Paris at the end of the 19th century when British designer Charles Frederick Worth created the first fashion brand with modern characteristics. Before that, wealthy customers would turn to specialist tailors for made-to-measure clothes, the style of which was dictated by the period's canons of *etiquette*. Worth was the first *couturier* in today's sense, the first to impose his own taste in clothing; a master in marketing and public relations, he was also the first to stage small fashion shows in which attractive young women, known as "sosies" (doubles), paraded in front of a very select clientele. This was the 19th century jet-setter fashionista elite, rigorously chosen by the eccentric designer. All the ingredients of contemporary fashion were already present in the 19th century: marketing, fashion shows, models, celebrities, elitism and, last but not least, a charismatic couturier to personify his brand.

Today, the fashion system has evolved extraordinarily, becoming one of the richest, most sophisticated, influential, creative and dynamic industries in the world, while retaining a distinctive allure of seduction and mystery. In step with changes in taste throughout history, and in addition to the evolution of fashion itself, shopping has undergone epochal transformations, to the point of becoming a daily activity, an integral part of everyone's life. The implications are not only of a practical nature; what we wear communicates who we are: clothes and accessories are aesthetic products, a means to define ourselves, they are objects of desire, cultural products of our time, albeit ephemeral and transitory.

Over the past decade, the internet has provided unprecedented access to fashion information, and e-commerce has radically changed the habits of millions of consumers. Today, we live in an era of widespread and rapid change, the market is dominated by a culture of immediate gratification, the very concept of seasonality, on which the fashion show calendar is based, has lost its *raison d'être* in the global panorama where the English winter is the Australian summer.

The issue of ethical and environmental sustainability, as well as the issue of inclusion, can no longer be ignored. As international trade intensified, the 21st century began with the demise of the West's uni-dimentional perspective. The whole system of production and consumption has been redefined: India and China are increasingly receptive markets, as are the Gulf countries and Russia. While the Western fashion system remains unshakeably attractive, new projects that arise from young designers' global vision are changing traditional structures. So what is it that creates the dream? What are the ingredients of fashion alchemy? How many aspects of the fashion universe are condensed into a single dress? The aim of this book is to take a look behind the scenes of a system that is as fascinating and creative as it is inextricably linked to strict commercial rules. Branding, marketing, history, cultural customs, communication and identity: fashion, style and the eternal search for beauty.

FASHION AND CONTEMPORANEITY

Fashion in the 20th and 21st centuries

Fashion is anything but frivolous: you can be obsessed with it, you can follow its dictates, you can deny it by declaring your disinterest... But the fact remains that every morning, in front of our wardrobes, each of us makes choices aimed at communicating a specific identity.

What we buy performs the delicate task of transforming us into an idealised version of ourselves: nowadays, more than ever, it is easy to imagine ourselves in someone else's shoes, in some other place; to conceive an image of ourselves that is different from the real one, concretising it via a series of objects that are available on an increasingly vast market. This is not only due to the relative distribution of wealth, it is more due to the fact that in today's society the consumer enjoys ever greater psychological and oneiric mobility [1].

The transition from the 20th to the 21st century was marked by epochal changes. Having abandoned the idealism of '68, we are witnessing a profound social change in which well-being and personal success replace family and community in the name of unbridled individualism. In fashion, the invention of prêt-à-porter stimulated demand for new garments on a regular basis and supply became more and more receptive to the needs of the new target customer: the young urban professional.

The decade from 1978 to 1988 laid the foundations for today's fashion system. Designers such as Ralph Lauren, Calvin Klein and Giorgio Armani created fashion business empires from scratch, at a speed that seemed impossible in the mid-1970s [2].

Calvin Klein figure, 1980s.

[1] Blumer, Klapp, 1960.
[2] Coleridge, 1988.

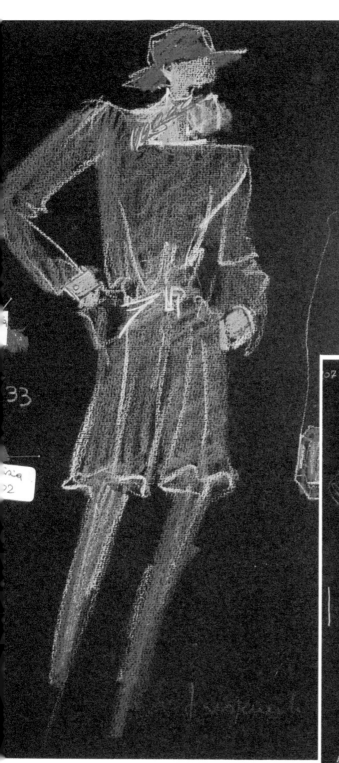

Armani, FW 1979-1980.

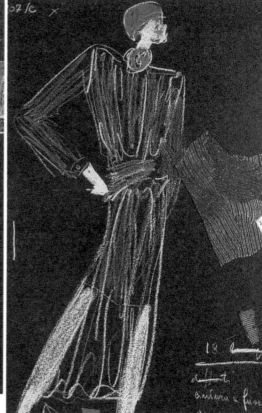

The new emphasis on marketing, advertising and the cult of personality, of celebrities and designers, led to a revolution in the industry that in part helped to shape the visual and cultural character of industrialised countries at the turn of the century. During that time, clothing had the power to communicate, and differences in terms of nationality, social status, gender and sexuality became blurred. And what emerges after a decade of dominating the trade press is a deliberate focus on the creativity of individuals – designers, models and elite consumers – as a form of contemporary mass spectacle [3].

At the end of the last century, glossy fashion magazines, together with designers and retailers, were still omnipresent forces that were capable of setting trends and guiding the tastes of thousands of people. In the West, Margareth Thatcher and Ronald Reagan's Liberalism promised to make people rich through speculation and financial mobility [4]. The years of the economic boom coincided with a marked increase in demand for quality *haute couture* and ready-to-wear garments.

Nouveau riche Americans and Middle Eastern oil princes entered the world of enthusiastic fashion buyers, bursting open the doors to new, hitherto little explored markets. In the 1980s, fashion was still strictly uni-directional [5], i.e., well-defined seasonal trends were presented on the catwalk (supported by a booming trade publishing industry) and followed en masse by consumers who were eager to look fashionable.

For the evening, the perfect socialite's wardrobe included structured, elaborately-decorated jackets and dresses from historic Parisian haute couture houses such as Balmain, Givenchy and Dior. For younger people, Mugler and Alaïa proposed tight mini dresses with laces and corsets.

Balmain figure, 1980s.

In 1983, Karl Lagerfeld was appointed Creative Director at Chanel, a cornerstone of classicism and elegance, and tasked with "modernising" the fashion house. Halfway between innovation and tradition, irony and sophistication, his approach won the favour of hundreds of new, enthusiastic young customers, while retaining the devotion of the company's traditional clientele who had always been faithful

[3] Breward, 1995, p. 226.
[4] Riello, 2012, p. 123.
[5] Laver, 2002, p. 273.

80s look, Karl Lagerfeld for
Chanel.

Christian Lacroix, 1988.

to the chic, casual elegance of the legendary bouclé wool suits. Thierry Mugler and Claude Montana's suits and jackets with padded shoulders, along with their "structured" blouses, reflected the new position of women in society: strong and independent, with a career of their own. Fashion would discover semiotics, along with Roland Barthes' theories, in the '60s, but it wouldn't be until the economic boom of the '80s, the glorification of personal success and money, that the turning point would present itself. Suddenly, the clothes took on new meanings within the effervescent urban culture. Deciphering a fashion show became a matter for experts, and the relationship between material clothing and an idea of Self in society became a push towards consumption.

An eccentric alternative to Western design was offered by the second wave of Japanese designers on the Paris catwalks, with Yohji Yamamoto and Rei Kawakubo of Comme des Garçons. Together with Kenzo Takada and Issey Miyake, who had been in Europe since the early '70s, they would present clothes based on layering, on wrapping the body in loose, unstructured garments.

THE 1990s

During the last decade of the 20th century, creativity reached new heights: fashion shows became theatrical performances and the biggest fashion brands gained international potency – the signature acquired central importance, the brand and its associated imagery triumphed.

In the '80s and '90s, Calvin Klein turned its name into a global brand: its jeans, perfumes and underwear, with the logo in plain sight, became symbolic products of a young and urban lifestyle. But the real pioneer of American fashion was Ralph Lauren (a master of branding in the modern sense), who transformed a small tie business into an empire built around the idea of a 1920s British aristocratic lifestyle. Not without a touch of glamour, it would become a symbol of an era in which lifestyle is more important than the product itself.

Lauren was adept at introducing the concept of lifestyle merchandising into his stores, offering customers an exclusive gentleman's club experience complete with aged oak panelling, dark leather armchairs and hammered brass fittings that shone in the warm lighting of the large American department stores [6]. For much of the 20th century, Parisian designers set the standards of fashion. Christian Dior's New Look, Coco Chanel's practical classicism, Balenciaga's baggy silhouette, Paco Rabanne's futuristic fashion and Yves Saint Laurent's ultra-feminine men's

Claude Montana, 1979.

[6] Agins, 1999, p. 87.

Within the image:
AMERICAN S

The mix of texture, subtle col
pieces... the base of
modern dressing at *CALVIN KI*

More Calvin Klein news: his make-up and fragrance collections — next month!

Like sliding on a wonderful silk bathrobe — and being dressed for dinner

At night: bareness, pretty color, shine . . . the works!

New basics: The V-neck dress! The shawl-collared linen jacket!

The ease of being in a skirt — of being in sportswear — today

The soft nutmeg colorings . . . the new narrow way to be in pants
All information, next to last page.

Linen/charmeuse/flannel: modern P.M. combination
Ishimuro

The pattern that makes crêpe de Chine look brand new (and with a textured sweater!)

Thin, thin suède and charmeuse . . . and in these colors!

174

Calvin Klein, *Vogue*, February 1978.

suit dictated fashion trends from the elite to the masses. But by the end of the last century, designers ceased to be arbiters of taste and glossy magazines lost their status as style bibles. For the first time, street style would enter haute couture ateliers: clothing sub-cultures from gothic to ethnic, from punk to grunge, became the primary source of inspiration for young designers. Brands such as Levi's, Nike and Gap appeared to be much more connected to everyday reality than the distant, idealised visions on the catwalk. The first half of the '90s saw the reintroduction of '60s and '70s revival styles, with futuristic looks, wedges, miniskirts, uniforms and sportswear. The vogue for retro styles led to vintage and second-hand clothing shops becoming very popular.

As the decade progressed, trends became even more mixed up and diversified. Sexy, minimalist, tailored and ethnic styles coexisted in the same season, in response to the

Thierry Mugler, Flower, SS 1982.

needs of an increasingly demanding clientele and the increasingly accentuated diversification of social activities.
The fashion industry became characterised by a mixture of
styles and references to the past. Designers became stylists who were skilled in reinterpreting classic shapes and
diverse styles, in order to meet the demands of an increas-

Federico Garolla

ingly differentiated, competitive market that was dependent as much on marketing as it was on creativity.

From the '90s onwards, the fashion industry lost its ability to set new trends, the sceptre of power passing into the hands of the consumer who, for the first time, could afford

Above: Yves Saint Laurent, 1978.
Right: the farewell parade, Centre
Georges Pompidou, Paris, 22nd
January 2002.

to decide where they wanted to buy any given product, as well as how they wanted to pay and how much they wanted to pay for it.

The Veblenian assumption that fashions originate in the elite sphere of haute couture and then trickle down to become mass consumption lost its relevance. Communication became global, the spread of the internet resulted in a new awareness of the world, the power of images transmitted non-stop from ubiquitous screens became universal.

From a commercial standpoint, improvements in communications and shipping technologies made global outsourcing more feasible around the turn of the century. Commercial exchanges reduced tariffs and other barriers to trade. And many once-poor nations integrated into the global economy, opening up new attractive markets for rich countries. China in particular generated a wave of affordable goods. With the advent of globalisation, the world would never be the same again.

The "made in China" season opens for fashion. Production was no longer necessarily confined to a specific place that was traditionally linked to a brand, but became delocalised to countries with low-cost labour. Production paradigms in the era of globalisation, which were mainly linked to cost-reduction projects based on traditional high-volume output schemes, applied to both luxury and low-cost brands. In this context, the assumption "you get what you pay for" failed.

The most diverse fashion, clothing and accessories became consumer goods that were within everyone's reach, at every price level, and the clear divide line between ordinary clothes and fashion with a capital "F" became increasingly blurred. It was then that mid- and low-priced chain stores began to colonise towns and shopping centres. Quality became an increasingly rare attribute, something that was difficult to find on the mass market, but was still taken into account. New generations quickly got used to cheap, mediocre tailoring, and were unable to distinguish between and appreciate different qualities of fabric and cuts.

In the age of visual communication, clothing and its tactile and sartorial quality takes a back seat in favour of identifiable signs of personal taste and spending power. The second half of the '90s saw the commercial triumph of must-have garments and accessories and the desire for ever-new purchases.

Primark, one of the best known low-cost clothing chains.

Then, riding the coattails of brands such as Gucci and Prada (who were the first to capitalise on bags, shoes and glasses featuring visible logos), along came Fendi with the iconic baguette. Pieces are often produced in small quantities so that their perceived scarcity on the market translates into a high level of desirability on the part of the customer, who is prepared to be added to stores' long waiting lists in order to obtain the coveted item.

THE 2000s

The beginning of the new millennium was marked by tragedy with the September 11 terrorist attack on the Twin Towers, on what would be the fourth day of New York Fashion Week for the spring/summer 2002 season. The fashion circus came to a halt, sets were evacuated and the remaining 73 shows were cancelled. For a few months, the fashion industry paused to reflect before storming back to business, stronger than ever. An ever-increasing number of designers, brands and retailers, as well as information that can communicate and sell to the world through the internet and new social media, are pouring into the fashion arena [7].

A market as global as it is competitive and overcrowded prompted designers and fashion houses to sharpen their weapons in order to assert their status and image. Since 2008, following the great financial crisis, it was marketing that siphoned billions in investments to please the new critical consumer. Creative in the face of evolving trends, the consumer was no longer conditioned by variations in income or social class, but was eclectic and pragmatic in terms of their own purchasing choices. The internet, which provides instant access to a wealth of information, makes the modern consumer increasingly sophisticated and demanding.

A simple logo is no longer enough to justify excessive expenditure. In addition to sensitivity to prices, there is a marked willingness to go crazy only when the purchase is guided by one of the four basic motivations that drive consumption in the new millennium [8]: personal gratification, establishing relationships, exploring new possibilities and expressing individual lifestyles according to a logic that is far removed from the mere display of shamelessly expensive clothes and accessories.

Emotional spaces that are linked to the product (which are indispensable in the definition of modern fashion brands) thereby come into play. The luxury sector in particular – which has evolved and expanded to include activities and lifestyles – would henceforth base its success on increasingly sophisticated communication strategies.

Jocelyn Morales on Unsplash

[7] Laver, 2012, p. 291.
[8] Silverstein, Fiske, 2004.

Laura Chouette on Unsplash

Outside fashion's ivory tower, these are dark days. In times of turbulent socio-economic conditions, nostalgia becomes a dominant cultural force. In the second decade of the 21st century, fashion moved in new directions to satisfy consumers' desires for ever-changing and individualistic looks.

No longer satisfied with big labels and tired of logos and it-bags, the fashion customer is constantly looking for original ideas to share on Instagram.

Fashion Brand. Luxury and High Street

The end of the millennium saw the absolute triumph of the brand, which arose from the need to segment, differentiate and distinguish products entering the consumer market in ever-increasing quantities [9].

According to Teri Agins, author of the famous essay *The End of Fashion*, it was precisely the utilitarian simplicity of '90s clothes that made marketing the sales tool par excellence in the fashion and luxury sectors. "Today's branding of fashion has taken on a critical role in an era when there's not much in the way of new styling going on - just about every store in the mall is peddling the same styles of clothes".

Previous to this, the consumer's attention was mainly focused on the product and its physical qualities; the brand was little more than a name [10]. But today, things have become decidedly more complicated: if you browse through the pages of newspapers, industry analyses and advertising in general, you will see that fashion and luxury are often intertwined.

In recent years, the horizon of high-end products has broadened to include the most diverse productions and experiences. From clothes to leather goods, eyewear, perfume, jewellery, restaurants, cars, hotels, wine and food... Goods and activities are used to communicate a lifestyle. For this reason, many of the companies operating in the fashion industry prefer to be included in the category related to the sale of lifestyle products rather than luxury.

[9] Riello, 2012, p. 123.
[10] Corbellini, Saviolo, 2007, p. 125.

This phenomenon is not new. At the beginning of the 20th century, legendary pioneer of contemporary fashion Paul Poiret not only freed women from the corset and dressed their bodies in exquisite Oriental-inspired creations, he also invented the concept of the catwalk, thereby elevating the status of clothing to a form of artistic expression.

Always in search of new ideas, *le magnifique* inaugurated the Martine atelier in 1912. The store was described by *Vogue* as "a place where it is possible to find everything that one could wish for, and each article is the loveliest of its kind". Products ranged from hand-painted glass bottles for perfume line Rosine, to silk parasols and larger items such as tables inlaid with coloured crystals. Much to Coco Chanel's *chagrin*, he would be the first French couturier to launch his own perfume. The first to realise that fashion could be promoted as a way of life. He would surround himself with artists, designers and architects who helped develop and promote his work.

This concept would be taken up again fifty years later by Christian Dior, whose gift lines were sold in sumptuous boutiques that were made to look like little palaces. By the end of the 1950s, Dior had licensed his name to produce lots of luxury accessories such as ties, hosiery, furs and bags, opening branches of the brand around the world.

When he burst onto the Paris fashion scene in 1947, his New Look created an unprecedented international frenzy, helping to usher a war-torn world into a new era of glamour and luxury. From a purely entrepreneurial point of view, the Dior fashion house was founded in 1946 with the capital of cotton magnate Monsieur Boussac. At that time, Louis Vuitton, Gucci and Cartier were still small family-owned companies whose business models were based on traditional dynamics on a local scale.

In the 1970s, despite the products' excellence, difficulties in coping with an expanding market beyond the borders of Europe made themselves felt. New capital and advanced organisational structures were needed to maintain international competitiveness. A key role in this phase was played by the Japanese market, driven by a demanding high-income clientele who considered Western products to be su-

Opposite: Paul Poiret, 1920.

Dior, HC SS 08.

perior in style and quality. Based on licensing agreements, business relations with Sol Levante serve to shed light on strategies adopted by European luxury manufacturers breaking into foreign markets. It was Japanese department stores such as Mitsukoshi, Takashimaya and Daimaru in particular that played a key role in spreading the concepts, "new", "modern" and "exclusive" [11], which from then on remained inextricably linked to European fashion.

LUXURY CENTRES

The 1980s saw the formation of the great French luxury centres, which became symbols of new Western capitalism on a global scale. Built up through multi-million euro acquisitions, renowned luxury conglomerates such as LVMH and

[11] Fujioka, R., Donzé. P.-Y., "European luxury big business and emerging Asian markets", 1960-2010-2015.

Ralph Lauren expands his lifestyle concept by extending it to coffee.

Kering now control a large part of the entire global luxury market. When he acquired Christian Dior in 1984, French entrepreneur with a passion for fashion Bernard Arnault was already on the crest of a wave. More than thirty years after the historic acquisition, Moët Hennessy Louis Vuitton, the group he founded, boasts a fabulous portfolio, with brands such as Celine, Dior, Fendi, Givenchy and of course Louis Vuitton.

Arnault's group is by far the largest of the large conglomerates, with around 60 brands that not only includes fashion, jewellery and cosmetics, but also wines and spirits, and had a market capitalisation of more than €200 billion in 2019, more than double that of Kering and Richemont.

In the late 1990s, the all-out war for control of Gucci ushered in a period where major fashion houses became listed companies with the obligation to guarantee and maintain stable and predictable growth for investors.

This takes the new capitalist dimension to a global scale, where free creativity – once the fashion industry's *raison d'être* – gives way to strict rules for making a profit. In 2001, after a bitter two-and-a-half year battle for the acquisition of the majority stake in the Gucci Group, Arnault and his alter ego François Pinault's companies reached a compromise that would see Pinault Printemps-Redoute (now Kering), secure absolute control of the Italian fashion house.

In the history of high-end fashion branding and fashion itself, Gucci's name marks the birth of an era in which marketing, branding and advertising budgets count as much as, if not more than, a designer's creativity. In the 1990s, Domenico de Sole (then CEO of the Gucci group) and Tom Ford (at the stylistic helm of the historic Florentine fashion house) understood better than anyone else before them that a fashion house's key to success lies not only in the quality of the clothes, but in the entire universe associated with the company itself.

With great skill and unscrupulousness, they were able to create a dream in which objects and values merged to convey a precise message, an ideal, a status, involving both psychological and emotional aspects.

90s advertising by Louis Vuitton
and Gucci.

LE SFUMATURE GUCCI

Theatrical fashion shows and high-profile advertising campaigns shot by photographic artists such as Richard Avedon, Steven Meisel, Helmut Newton, and curated by Carine Roitfeld (future editor of *Vogue France*), transformed the sober brand on the verge of bankruptcy into a sexy, daring and highly-coveted successful brand. The redefinition of the entire Gucci aesthetic in communications and retailing, as well as the reinterpretation of the fashion house's classic stylistic elements, caused sales of products with higher profit margins to surge.

Shoes, bags, belts and eyewear became iconic objects of desire within the reach of the wider society. In terms of influence and sales, the power of accessories became one of the indicative factors that would influence the direction that fashion would take at the dawn of the 21st century, a reality that is now well established.

The connection between luxury and lifestyle is now more popular than ever, thanks to legions of consumers who are eager to purchase special and authentic products, items that are capable of enriching their lives by conveying uniqueness and distinction. In the case of luxury brands, a brand's distinctive features have come to signify not only quality, but also specific ideas in the consumer's mind about the prestige and appeal of the product.

Chanel's double "C" is not just a brand; it reminds us of Paris, beautifully dressed ladies, tailor-made suits, quilted bags and red carpets [12]. These images help articulate brand identity, successfully creating a sense of elitist lifestyle.

Associating a brand with a specific lifestyle is a slow and evolutionary process that requires patience, attention and the skilful use of images that tell stories beyond the product. Messages and images are not only broadcast through traditional magazines and advertisements but also across multiple channels, including blogs, social media profiles and interactive apps.

[12] Riello, McNeil, 2016, p. 262.

Chanel's iconic double "C" on the end of a lipstick.

Fast fashion revolution

Fashion is often superficially labelled as the poster industry for consumerist materialism. It is seen as being based on frivolous, trivial and ephemeral logic, shaped by unlimited consumption and the mass production of superfluous items; a highly polluting industry linked to abuses of workers' rights. Yet fashion occupies a special place at the heart of contemporary culture; it provides jobs for millions of people worldwide, and represents an opportunity for creativity and mutual communication.

Fast fashion has raised controversy in recent years, and has completely changed our approach to clothing and the way consumers shop. The specific type of production and distribution methods made known globally by brands such as Zara and H&M means fashion items can be sold at record speed and at affordable prices. The reality is that fast fashion is just a term given to a constantly evolving system of production that has its roots in the late 18th century, during the era of the first industrial revolution.

The invention of textile machines leads to garments being made in factories on a large scale and in standardised sizes. Patented in 1846, the sewing machine would itself play an extraordinary role in the history of clothing and fashion over the last 150 years. A prodigious piece of industrial machinery, its use rapidly spread to domestic settings, which not only caused a sharp fall in clothing prices but also gave a strong boost to the production of everyday garments.

While the famous haute couture houses served the elite of the nobility and upper middle class, and the local tailoring firms dressed middle-class women, the lower income brackets continued to make their own clothes at home. Family-run tailoring workshops typically included a small group of employees with some aspects of production outsourced to home-based workers for very low wages [13].

Although this type of operation was mostly carried out locally, the practice of using an organisational system called sweated labour, along with the exploitation of labour in the 19th century, provides a small taste of what would become the underlying principle of most modern apparel production a century later. Working at home without social protections, instead of in a factory, has been a cornerstone of the fast fashion supply chain for years.

Today it is particularly prevalent in countries such as India, Bangladesh, Vietnam and China, where millions of low-income domestic workers, mostly women, children and immigrants work piece-work for very low wages.

At the beginning of the 20th century, despite the growing number of factories and technical innovations, most clothing production still took place at home or in small workshops. The world wars led to fabric being rationed. This led to styles becoming more functional, and production for all garments was standardised.

[13] Breward, 2003.

A sweatshop from the early 20th century.

While wartime restrictions in the 1950s made middle-class consumers more aware of the purchase value of mass-produced clothing, it was during the 1960s that fashion trends began to change abruptly. The younger generations' rejection of tailoring traditions gave rise to an insatiable thirst for new garments at affordable prices.

The world of informal and young people's clothing exploded in both Europe and the United States: in England, with Mary Quant's revolutionary miniskirt and swinging London and in the United States with the legendary jeans worn by James Dean [14]. To keep up with the growing demand for low-priced clothes and accessories, fashion brands moved production to large factories abroad – first in China, a business move that allowed Western companies to save billions of euros by outsourcing labour.

[14] Saviolo, Testa, 2012.

Nothing in contemporary culture reflects the modern consumer's thirst for instant gratification purchases like the fashion industry does. This is a characteristic that has enabled many of the companies we know today as leaders in the fast fashion industry to make huge profits.

Starting off as small shops in Spain, Sweden, England and Ireland, the brands Zara, H&M, Topshop and Primark began their ascent around the middle of the 20th century, seeping into the international market around the 1990s and 2000s.

While until the 1980s the average consumer was willing to buy expensive designer clothes as a guarantee of lasting quality, the second decade of the 21st century saw the motivation to buy fast fashion arise from a desire to constantly have new (but cheaper and poor quality) replicas of fashionable items seen on the catwalk.

In the wake of the great success of low-cost fashion in the early 2000s, retailers in the industry aimed to increase profits by focusing on key elements of the supply chain, with an emphasis on increasing the speed of production, for a rapid turnover of goods at ever lower prices.

This strategic ability to always introduce new collections based on the latest trends quickly saw Zara triumph. Its founder, Amancio Ortega, opened his first shop in northern Spain in 1975, guided by the same principle that characterises the brand today: to sell garments inspired by haute couture at affordable prices in record time.

When Zara arrived in New York in the early 1990s, the *New York Times* used the term fast fashion to describe the store's mission: "At Zara, too, the emphasis is on fast fashion, merchandised in a coordinated style... It would only take 15 days for a garment to go from a designer's brain to being sold on the racks". In the late 1990s and early 2000s it became increasingly socially acceptable to declare one's love for low-cost fashion. The new eclectic and pragmatic consumer casually frequents both low-priced fashion shops and boutiques in the city centre, mixing "high and low" in search of making maximum savings and buying superior products.

Left: Mary Quant, 1965.
Right: clothing by Mary Quant, 1967.

When the first H&M store opened on New York's Fifth Avenue in April 2000, the *New York Times* published an article declaring: "It's chic to pay less", highlighting the Swedish fast chain's prodigious timing in seizing the emerging trend among consumers to abandon the classic department store in favour of bargain hunting.

Today, the traditional fast fashion brands that base their business on physical shops have been joined by new names operating exclusively online. Asos and FashionNova, in particular, offer lines directly inspired by catwalk looks or those worn by stars, a highly successful business model that focuses on speed and the ability to pick up on new trends, reworking them in an ultra-affordable version.

In recent years, public figures such as Kate Middleton and Michelle Obama have helped to definitively clear the way for low-cost style. Both the Duchess of Cambridge and the wife of the former President of the United States have cleverly used fashion as a visual language, connecting with the masses regardless of social and economic contexts.

Fast fashion at affordable prices appeals to everyone; the widespread practice of self-expression through clothing choices has had an impact on contemporary social dynamics that is far from insignificant. Without forgetting the advantages (in terms of jobs and economic development), the negative environmental impact linked to the overproduction and disposal of garments considered to be perishable disposable goods remains serious and evident.

The thirst for new cheap clothes also creates an ethical problem regarding the conditions of the workers involved in production. Often, factories are located in countries like China, Bangladesh, Vietnam and other major apparel export centres, where labels have little oversight over working conditions, let alone copyright violations. Garment workers in factories around the world – most of whom are women – are often poorly paid and work in abusive conditions.

In addition to exploitative practices, the fast fashion industry (valued at around US$2.5 trillion in 2018), is causing an unprecedented environmental emergency.

In addition to being one of the largest global users of water, the fast fashion industry produces a large amount of waste due to the constant turnover of goods. Textile waste is an unintended consequence of fast fashion: millions of garments thrown away like rubbish filling up landfills, where the synthetic compounds from which the fibres are made can take hundreds or thousands of years to biodegrade.

Vibrant colours, prints and fabric finishes are key features of fashion garments, but many of them are made with toxic chemicals.

Textile dyeing is the second largest polluter of clean water globally after agriculture. Wardrobes in developed countries are full to bursting, and in order to sell more products, retailers must tempt their customers with a constant stream of new items. This is a radical change in mentality compared to not so many years ago, when a garment was bought to last for years.

Eras, places and fashion.
Fashion capitals, fashion shows, street style

For several years now, the flashy fashion weeks in New York, London, Milan and Paris have been accompanied by rumours announcing the end of fashion shows. However, despite the criticism, it is hard to imagine doing without the event that best celebrates the spirit of fashion par excellence.

For over a century, the world of fashion has been rigidly divided into four seasons: spring, summer, autumn and winter. Over time, the shows have evolved from an exclusive in house presentation of haute couture for a private clientele, to a biannual media event of couture and ready-to-wear clothing with a global reach.

Underlying this evolution are both cultural and social forces, including increased consumer awareness of fashion as a direct means of self-expression, the rise of the prêt-à-porter industry after World War II, the growth of designers' and models' media prominence, and a greater attention paid to the catwalks by the popular press.

Valentino fashion show, SS 08.

Design by Charles Frederick Worth, ca.1900.

Today's fashion show is quite different to its early 20th century incarnation, but it retains important links to its origins in its theatrical staging and connotation as a couture show.

From the time of Louis XIV, France was considered to be the centre of diffusion for all fashions. Every year, with regularity, the major courts in European capitals awaited the arrival of "fashion dolls", inanimate emissaries [15] of transalpine fashion dressed according to the latest trends of the French court.

A diffusion dynamic was linked to court *etiquette*, which was in vogue at least until the end of the 19th century, when English designer (Parisian by choice), Charles Frederick Worth began to design and make clothes for high society and had them paraded on the catwalk, worn by real models. Until then, the idea of a tailor-as-creator did not exist: Worth was the first to achieve the rank of creator, the first

[15] Gnoli, 2015, p. 13.

couturier in the modern sense. With him, the very concept of haute couture was born: exclusive garments for a limited clientele, available seasonally and promoted by means of spectacular catwalks.

Today, haute couture fashion represents the purest creative soul of the fashion industry, a space of excellence where creativity and craftsmanship set the rules.

Haute couture is showcased twice a year in Paris, where a handful of brands make hand-made clothes to order, costing from €10,000 to over €100,000 a piece.

To qualify as a couture house, which is an official designation like Champagne, a brand must maintain an atelier of a certain number of full-time artisans and produce a specific number of garments per year.

Today, very few brands are able to meet the requirements; among the greats are Chanel, Christian Dior, Valentino, Armani Privé, Atelier Versace, Giambattista Valli, Schiaparelli.

Many, including Saint Laurent, have left the industry over the years, while the Fédération Française de la Couture, which governs high fashion standards, has loosened some of its strict rules to admit young designers with fewer resources.

Newcomers include names such as Dutch designer Iris van Herpen and Chinese designer Guo Pei, best known for designing the Yellow Empress "omelette" dress worn by pop star Rihanna at the Met Gala in 2015. Only a few hundred customers in the world regularly buy couture, but the clothes made for haute couture lines are also worn by international stars on red carpets in order to promote the brand image.

While in the late 1900s fashion shows were still private, informal affairs that usually included models casually walking among small groups of customers, by the 1910s they became increasingly popular events. The first atelier shows could last up to three hours and were repeated several times a day over the course of several weeks [16].

[16] Evans, C., "The Enchanted Spectacle. Fashion Theory", vol. 5, n. 3, 2001, pp. 271-310.

Rihanna in the Yellow Empress
dress by Guo Pei, Met Gala 2015.

At the time, the models on the catwalk were introduced by design-related numbers to help customers better identify their chosen outfit. It wasn't until the end of the decade that, due to an increasing number of foreign buyers flocking to Europe to catch up on the latest trends, fashion houses began to schedule their shows on fixed dates, twice a year depending on the season, laying the foundations for what we now call Fashion Week.

By the time Christian Dior made his debut with his groundbreaking Corolle collection in 1947, fashion shows had already become a full-blown affair. Large-scale media events were advertised and hosted in stylists' lounges or in small, designer locations. Beautiful, statuesque professional models replaced the informal walkabout style of the past. The seated audience was crammed into small rooms, along with famous journalists lined up in the front row, and retail buyers and potential customers scattered here and there [17].

[17] Evans, 2001.

By the mid-1950s, many high-end department stores on both sides of the ocean regularly scheduled fashion shows to promote their image. The traditional format of the fashion show was completely revolutionised in the 1960s, coinciding with the rise of ready-to-wear and the gradual decline of couture.

Discreet and relatively solemn, haute couture presentations were replaced by energetic shows in unusual locations, with designers such as Mary Quant and André Courrèges encouraging their models to abandon the traditional catwalk setting and embrace fluid and more natural movements [18].

Instead of wooing the press and shoppers with an aura of luxury and exclusivity, designers, directly influenced by savvy marketing techniques, would henceforth use fashion shows as a means to connect with the masses, stimulate consumption and not least to embrace the emerging youth culture.

By the 1980s, fashion shows had become so popular that, in 1984, "fashion showman" Thierry Mugler organised a colossal public catwalk at the Zénith stadium in Paris. A crowd of 6000 people including paying guests, accredited journalists and buyers from all over the world attended the show, during which the models gave life to cartoons on themes including the Olympics, the space age and religion. The production was worthy of a film set, culminating in the angelic appearance of Pat Cleveland as the Madonna.

Other designers have pushed the idea of a fashion show far beyond the confines of a traditional runway. On 12th July 1998, France won the football World Cup, but an hour before kick-off, an extraordinary retrospective show with 300 models took place at the Stade de France on live television to celebrate forty years of fashion by Yves Saint Laurent. In more recent years, few designers have stood out on the catwalk as much as the late Alexander McQueen, known for turning his shows into human chessboards and wind tunnels. Events fall somewhere between fashion and performance, art and commerce.

[18] Steele, 2004.

Christian Dior, Corolle line, 1947.

Although many designers have staged shows in exotic locations and original settings, Karl Lagerfeld is perhaps the designer who has elevated the fashion show to levels that would have turned *Mademoiselle* Chanel's head. Over the years, Lagerfeld has presented his collections for the French fashion house in grandiose locations that were designed to resemble surreal brasseries, airport terminals and supermarkets: settings that fall halfway between the catwalk and everyday life.

In 2017, he even transformed the Great Wall of China into a catwalk for Fendi with 500 VIP guests, escorted by plane to attend the monumental event.

At the dawn of the new millennium, the term catwalk entered popular vocabulary as a synonym for style and glamour. The days when a fashion show was just a procession of models holding up numbered cards as they walked through quiet rooms among buyers and journalists, are now a thing of the past. But beyond the choice of location and the level of spectacle, the biggest change to the way clothes have been exhibited over the last four decades is seen in the models themselves.

With the disappearance of the submissive "mannequins" employed by traditional couture salons, from the 1970s onwards it was charismatic characters such as Jerry Hall and Pat Cleveland who would conquer the scene. The triumph of the supermodel phenomenon reached its peak in March 1991, when Gianni Versace paraded Naomi Campbell, Christy Turlington, Linda Evangelista and Cindy Crawford together to the tune of George Michael's "Freedom".

Today, although there are many fashion weeks around the world, only four (Paris, Milan, London and New York) are recognised as official. One of the criticisms expressed by the press and those working in the industry is that fashion shows have become events for their own sake: extravagant spectacles where clothes, once the undisputed stars, have slipped into the background in favour of celebrities and breathtaking staging.

In a market that is extremely complex, the role of the catwalk show in the construction of a brand's identity is now more important than ever, especially in the upper echelons of fashion. More and more, fashion week is becoming a pure marketing exercise, where the perception of the brand counts more than the cut of its dresses.

For designers and companies, it's about gaining attention in an environment that has never been as overcrowded and confusing as it is today. Fast fashion has only complicated matters by teaching consumers to compulsively buy cheap, trendy clothing. This, among other factors – in-

Opposite
Above: Alexander McQueen bids farewell to his audience during the FW 2009-2010 fashion show in Paris.
Below: Karl Lagerfeld, Chanel fashion show, 1991.

Fendi fashion show, organised by Karl Lagerfeld at the Great Wall of China, 2017.

cluding the cost of maintaining production excellence that is both ethical and of high quality, along with fierce competition from new brands from all four corners of the globe – has made catwalk fashion a difficult thing to sell. It is therefore completely understandable that fashion brands are bending over backwards in an attempt to remain relevant in the eyes of an increasingly demanding and eclectic clientele.

The recent trend towards larger shows has the practical purpose of promoting the licensing and sale of cheaper products, such as fragrances or sunglasses, which alone account for a significant part of a fashion house's revenue.

Gone are the days when only magazine editors, socialites and insiders celebrated fashion week. Thanks to Instagram, Snapchat, live feeds and blogs capturing images from the catwalk across the internet in real time, anyone can watch the show. The old advertising model has been replaced by incessant web traffic and numbers generated by social media; in this context, impactful visual and viral information has gained central importance. Even in terms

Supermodels in a Versace advert, 1992.

of casting, new models such as Kendall Jenner and Gigi Hadid are selected according to their respective number of followers.

For a long time now, the staging of extravagant shows in major fashion cities has often included a street style circus. Aspiring influencers in flashy outfits and unlikely combinations in search of visibility flock to the main catwalk locations. A show within a show that has become a tired cliché, but which in the past has shed light on skilful street photographers, who have now entered the highest ranks of fashion photography.

Conceived as social and communication events, one will often see the latest poster child, celebrities, music stars and bloggers – those who in marketing jargon are called influencers – sitting in the front row of a fashion show. Ordinary folks comment on and wear clothing made by fashion houses, and thanks to followers and engagement, this should induce the general public to go out and buy these clothes and accessories, or at least make them more desirable.

Street style.

Fashion editors vs influencers.
Fashion in old and new media

Newspapers and magazines play a major role in the dissemination of fashion. This is a story that begins way back in 1678, when Parisian publisher Donneau de Visé included an illustrated description of contemporary French fashion (complete with the names of the suppliers) in his women's magazine *Mercure Galant* for the first time. While in the 18th century the few magazines on the market were still only intended for an ambitious and wealthy readership, by the mid-19th century the readership multiplied and periodicals even became accessible to the middle class.

Thanks to technological progress, increased circulation and greater use of images, magazines became more and more attractive to advertisers. The first advertising agency was founded in 1890 and, from then on, the advertising and publishing empires we know today began to flourish.

At the beginning of the 20th century, one of the most important personalities in the world of contemporary publishing

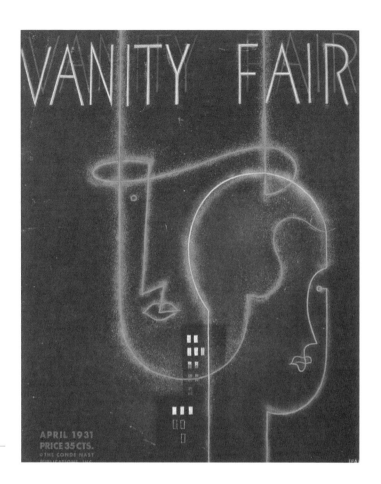

Cover of *Vanity Fair*, 1931.

appeared on the scene: William Randolph Hearst. Owner of several newspapers in the United States, Hearst engaged in a battle for the last reader, a challenge he won thanks to the contribution of his mentor Joseph Pulitzer.

Since its founding on 4th March 1887, the Hearst publishing house has gone from owning a single newspaper to being one of the world's leading private media and information companies. First published in 1898, *Harper's Bazaar* magazine is a reference point for the diffusion of fashion in the modern sense, in part thanks to the direction of the legendary Diana Vreeland, at the helm of the magazine from 1936 to 1962. Thirty years earlier, *Vanity Fair* was founded in England.

These were the days when Manhattan became the birthplace of a new generation of graphic designers, art directors and editors, who brought about the idea of the fusion of designer advertising and glossy magazines as we know it today. Legendary editors such as Carmel Snow and Diana Vreeland (director of *Harper's Bazaar* since 1936), worked in skyscrapers in the heart of New York; by 1963, Vreeland had become editor-in-chief at *Vogue America*.

The ability to reproduce high-quality images in print allowed readers to peek into the luxurious apartments and homes of the rich and famous. This was Diana Vreeland's great innovation at *Vogue America* in the early 1960s [19]. Thanks to Horst P. Horst's lush colour photography and the sharp journalism of his partner Valentine Lawford, this made elite fashion more desirable and sought-after than ever.

As the speed of fashion increased, the industry's publishing scene drew new momentum from the developments of *Women's Wear Daily*. By 1972, its offshoot *W*, developed by John Fairchild, was conceived with the idea of having "the speed of a newspaper... with the smart look of a fashion magazine" and – significantly – its survival depended on advertising.

Designed to encourage a desire for tailoring on an ever-increasing scale, the specialised periodical press would experience its golden age in the late 19th and early 20th centuries.

The rapid and far-reaching changes associated with the rise of celebrities as style leaders, the spectacular new dimension assumed by the fashion industry and the immense proliferation of luxury consumer goods would have mattered little without the publicity generated by the mass-produced images and texts that accompanied them [20].

Today, as then, although with completely different dynamics, the fashion industry depended on the consolidated power of graphic communication and the potential of visual reproduction as a means to transform a simple garment into a visual product, to be sold and discussed.

The economic crisis of 2008 would later mark the slow decline of the glossy magazine as an exclusive means of communicating fashion to the masses. Increasingly dependent

[19] Riello, McNeil, 2016.

[20] Breward, 2011, p. 115.

Glossy magazine covers.

on advertising, even in terms of journalistic content, the conventional magazine has lost its authority over the years.

The pace and fruition of fashion itself has accelerated so much that the traditional "lead in" time for a quality colour service – which usually takes weeks to process – is now too long to keep up with changing trends and the needs of an increasingly eclectic and sophisticated clientele.

In the first weeks of 2009, the prospects of fashion publishers such as Condé Nast, which has almost monopolised the high-end magazine sector over the years, looked decidedly bleak. In response to the recession, advertisers began to cut back on marketing expenditure. As a result, the number of advertising pages – the barometer of a magazine's health – dropped dramatically.

Many newspapers began to cut their budgets, others immediately tried the online route, but the idea of magazines migrating online still remains a controversial issue today, not least because the current business model underlying online publishing is not yet totally self-sufficient.

All this while an increasing number of fashion blogs and other online start-ups produce their own content at low cost. The arrival of the blogger in particular has undermined the foundations of the old establishment of admired fashion editors. Historically, characters – often from high society – would make their way into the right salons and with an impeccable sense of style. At the same time as democratic fashion emerged, blogging helped to make the elitist spirit associated with many glossy magazines somewhat out-dated, to say the least.

The easiest way to describe a blogger is "someone who is known primarily for their website". This could be photo-based work, such as that of Tommy Ton or *The Sartorialist*, or perhaps written articles, such as those by Susannah Lau of *Style Bubble* and Chiara Ferragni of *The Blonde Salad*. Emerging for the first time over a decade ago, the blogger marked a huge milestone in terms of democratising the fashion industry. Fashion bloggers have a point of view, a certain taste and a unique way of presenting and documenting fashion, both visually and in written form. Those who have been most successful have been able to monetise their content in terms of advertising, campaigns and brand sponsorships. Some of them have risen to the rank of influencers due to the large number of followers accumulated on various social media.

Like the "it girls" of the past, the best known influencers are paid to attend fashion shows, designer dinners and events. Currently, the value of an influencer is rooted in the number and type of their followers, data that translates into advertising appeal and influence in terms of purchasing decisions. Historically, the top editors of the most exclusive magazines would occupy the front row as an indicator of their importance. Nowadays, however, it is common to find Anna Wintour sitting next to the latest influencer or blogger.

The rise of influencers has benefited brands who have found in them yet another profitable marketing opportunity.

In a new world where the formula for success is no longer as clear-cut as it once was, no single entity has had such a lasting effect on the fashion ecosystem as the photo-sharing service launched by Apple on 6th October 2010: Instagram.

The photo-sharing app, which was acquired by Facebook for US$1 billion in 2012, is where people now turn to discover new trends and to shop. In June 2018, the Californian company surpassed one billion users per month. As fewer and fewer readers buy traditional magazines on newsstands, brands have responded by following consumers online and shifting their marketing budgets from print to social media networks.

FASHION AND SOCIAL SCIENCES: "I BUY THEREFORE I AM"

Beyond the clothes themselves.
The meaning of fashion in society

Fashion is not just about dressing well. It is a reflection of history, culture and social change. It is much more than just an expression of sentiment.

Fashion fosters novelty and individuality, aspects that stimulate economic production and consumption.

Fashion is a mix of conformity and individual choice, its centrality in everyday experience remains undeniable: "being fashionable", being indifferent to it or claiming to reject its practice is now the norm for affirming social and personality differences. Perhaps more than in the past, where its whims, extravagances and transformations were the exclusive prerogative of the wealthy classes, today's fashion logic claims a central place in any analysis of contemporary culture.

The study of its social dynamics goes back at least three centuries: few philosophers have investigated its *raison d'être*, few economists have highlighted its financial significance; many sociologists and psychologists have tried to understand the sense of ambivalence associated with it.

For centuries seen as a frivolous and trivial vice, good only for dullards and layabouts, fashion – understood as an extravagance, a display of wealth and a disturbance of the social order – has aroused criticism and given rise to laws preventing ostentation and consumption.

Fashion reflects the frenetic pace in which we live, our obsession with progress and novelty. Objects, goods – especially clothes and the clothing industry – are recognised as fundamental in modern democracies. It is not just about the defining elements within a society: the consumerism of clothing – albeit with its many dark sides – is seen as tangible proof of individual freedom of expression through appearance.

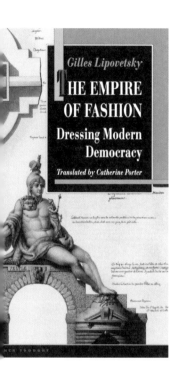

In his book *The Empire of Fashion*, controversial social philosopher Gilles Lipovetsky shows how the evolution of fashion, from privilege for the upper class to a vehicle of popular expression, closely follows the rise of democratic values. According to Lipovetsky, fashion is a reflection of the modern cult of appearance and actually serves the common good. Today's mass-produced fashion promises many choices, which in turn allow consumers to become "complex individuals within a stable and democratically-educated society".

But let's take a step back in time. Between the 1600s and the first half of the 1900s, various theses were put forward on the phenomenon of fashion. With very few exceptions, a feeling of condemnation, impatience and often rejection emerges. The range of studies is vast, so I will limit myself to summarising the best known contributions. In the second half of the 17th century, French philosopher Jean de La Bruyère spoke of "subservience to fashion" as an "unreasonable thing".

In 1705, Bernard de Mandeville, a Dutch physician living in London, anonymously published *The Fable of the Bees*. In the poem, Mandeville describes a community of bees that thrive until they are suddenly made honest and virtuous. Without the desire for personal gain, their economy collapses and the surviving bees lead a simple life in a small hollow tree.

The moral of the story? Without private vices, there is no public benefit. Consequently, "fashion and luxury, the fruit of pride and vanity, can ruin a private individual, but they are the greatest promoters of commerce, always enriching a well-managed state". Among the best-known sources is the legendary *Encyclopédie* by Diderot and d'Alembert, the first seven volumes of which were published between 1751 and 1784. It includes over three thousand entries

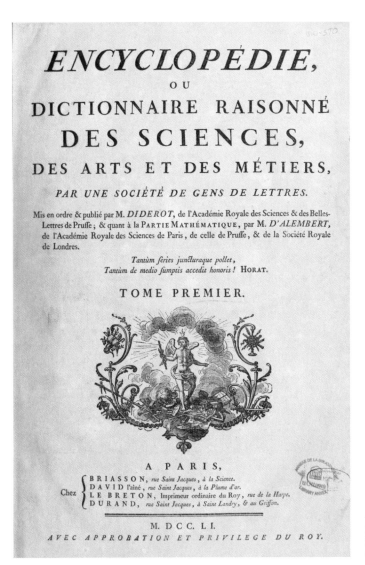

on the theme of fashion. The Marquis of Saint-Lambert coined the term "luxury" as meaning "the use of wealth and industry to achieve a pleasurable lifestyle. Luxury stems primarily from our lack of satisfaction with our situation, our desire to feel better than we do. This desire is the cause of men's passions, their virtues and their vices". And he continues: "Luxury exists at all social levels, in all societies: the savage has a hammock that he buys with animal hides; the European has his sofa, his bed. Our wives wear red and diamonds. In Florida, women wear blue, and glass beads".

Of all the philosophers, perhaps the most influential of all was the Frenchman Jean-Jacques Rousseau. In *The Confessions*, published posthumously in 1782, he tells us in great detail about his way of dressing and his relationship with clothes. After his first literary successes, by which time he had been following trends for quite some time, he decided to dress according to "what was good and reasonable for himself" so as not to be subject to the opinion of others. "I gave up gilding and white stockings, took to wearing a round wig, put down the sword and sold watches".

Like the other Enlightenment thinkers, Rousseau found fashion to be a negative phenomenon, the child of boredom and vanity. According to him, women should never dress too gaudily: "A beautiful dress can make you shine, but what is really attractive is the person; excessive ornaments makes you look ridiculous".

A form of vanity and madness, according to Immanuel Kant, fashion is not a matter of taste, but of simple vanity that lies in the desire for distinction and competition in the will to outdo each other (*Pragmatic Anthology*).

Friedrich Nietzsche proves to be even more severe. For the famous German philosopher, fashion is defined as "the form of the many", it is the slave's "misunderstanding" about beauty, a misunderstanding that fascinates men and women with a servile mentality, based on imitation and apishness. Its changeability is an indication of the men's and women's immaturity, of their stupidity and vulgarity.

Nietzsche does, however, recognise a not insignificant advantage of fashions, namely their ability to procure "self-confidence and mutual cheerful agreeableness to those who know they are all bound by its law" [1].

A complex and brilliant writer, Walter Benjamin is the art world's favorite theorist. According to him, fashion – like the arts – anticipates the future and for this reason should represent a "burning interest" for philosophers and theorists: "Every season carries in its latest creations a secret sign of things to come. Whoever were to learn to read these signs would not only know something of the new artistic trends, but also of new codes, wars, revolutions" [2].

[1] Nietzsche, 1970, p. 75.

[2] Benjamin, 1986, p. 111.

But it wouldn't be until the second half of the 19th centu-ry that fashion, hand in hand with industrialisation, would become the business of many. It was during this time that the close relationship between clothing and social situa-tion emerged. In this context, therefore, it would be the so-ciologists, with their fledgling discipline eager to explain evolving institutions, who would make an enlightened con-tribution to understanding the fashion phenomenon. Be-tween imitation and the search for distinctive individuality, between status and novelty at all costs, sociologists' the-ses, unlike those of philosophers, do not blame or make hasty condemnations.

For decades on the fringes of the social sciences, it was thanks to a growing number of academic journals and pub-lications that fashion gradually gained respect as a research topic. It was classical sociologists who laid the foundations of a theoretical framework that would later be diversified into a variety of contemporary fashion theories.

Classical fashion discourse owes its fame to scholars such as Herbert Spencer, Ferdinand Tönnies, Thorstein Veblen and Georg Simmel. They all shared a common view: fashion is about the process of imitation [3].

Imitators are people at the lower end of the social spec-trum, while those who are imitated sit at the top. This is the fundamental principle of the hugely popular "cascade" fashion theory, later called Herbert Blumer's "class differ-entiation theory".

We need only think of 17th and 18th century Europe, when the nobility dictated habits, lifestyle and clothing. Lifestyles and fashions were imitated by the rising bourgeoisie, who were eager to acquire status and privileges. The common people had to make do with a few rags or traditional cos-tumes that had remained unchanged for centuries, indiffer-ent to fashion.

Among the most cited theorists, American sociologist and economist Thorstein Veblen, author of the famous book *The Theory of the Leisure Class: An Economic Study of Institutions*, introduces fashion within the creation and institutionalisa-tion of the wealthy class through the activity of consumption.

The newspaper of families, 1867.

[3] *International Journal of Arts, Humanities and Social Studies*, vol 2, n. 5, September-October 2020, pp. 16-22.

MODE DI PARIGI

Milano, da Alessandro Lampugnani editore.

GIORNALE DELLE FAMIGLIE

In short, Veblen saw fashion as an expression of the wearer's wealth. Clothes and accessories are an immediate indication of an individual's spending power. German sociologist and philosopher Georg Simmel shares Spencer and Veblen's opinion, and goes further to say that fashion is a form of "imitation and social equalisation", which changes incessantly.

The elite initiate fashion but, when the masses imitate it in an attempt to erase or weaken social distinctions, the elite then abandon it for a newer style – a process that accelerates as wealth increases. For Simmel, fashion was not just clothing, but a central process in the shaping of modern society. Any object can represent fashion, be it clothes, ideas or habits, but in essence he "refers to any field of social action in which there is a dynamic process, somewhere between individual affirmation and integration".

The 19th century discourse on fashion, which is still so popular today, is mainly linked to the concept of imitation. For some, fashion is characteristic of democratic societies, while for others it remains an expression of class distinction. Classical theories converge on the idea that fashion is always created "from above", by renowned designers in the "grand ateliers".

They see elite fashion as something that trickles down to the middle classes and then further down the social ladder to the masses. This theory seem to fit the current *raison d'être* of fast fashion, which has repeatedly been accused of copying ideas from the catwalks and translating them into poor imitations that are then made available on the market for a fraction of the price. Then there is the contemporary obsession with the rich and famous whose images circulate on social media, generating staggering sales when the Meghan Markle of the day decides to wear a dress by whatever brand, whether it is well-known or not.

In the 20th century, as social barriers fell, many sociologists opposed this view, arguing that fashion is not a product of differentiation and emulation of the upper classes, but a response to the desire to be up-to-date and to express new tastes in a constantly changing world. Today's fashion implies fluidity and mobility, and requires a particular ter-

Gustave Caillebotte, *Paris Street; Rainy Day*, 1877.

rain in order to thrive and disseminate – namely the modern world, where social structures are open and flexible.

There must be differences in social positions, but it must seem possible, as well as desirable, to bridge this gap. This is the mechanism on which big luxury brands focus, with promises of success and admiration within arm's reach according to the Gospel of Marketeers, through the purchase of goods and services that confer status. With his notion of taste as a key element of social identity, Pierre Bourdieu argued that in contemporary society we are increasingly judged on our appearance. The clothes a man wears, the language he speaks and the manners he displays carry more weight in conferring social esteem than his character or morals.

As Gillo Dorfles wrote, today there is a "realisation of how rapidly an osmosis is being reached between lifestyle and clothing style. Between the way of conceiving existence and the way of presenting oneself to others." [4].

Just as the term and the very concept of "class" is now considered completely "unfashionable", so modern theories have rejected the idea of the fundamental importance of imitation in the process of diffusing trends. According to scholars, American Herbert Blumer was probably the first to reject the idea of imitation and class differentiation in fashion.

His ideas were put forward by several contemporary sociologists. René König, Elizabeth Wilson and Fred Davis explored fashion as a modern phenomenon that is characterised by mobility within a flexible social system.

The importance of the consumer first came into the picture thanks to the insights of American sociologist Diana Crane, who demonstrated how the social meaning of clothing had been radically transformed in the space of a hundred years.

Whereas in the 19th century it was social class – reflected in clothing – that determined a person's identity, by the end of the 20th century it was lifestyle, gender, sexual orientation, age and ethnicity that determined fashion choices. Leisure clothes, in particular, "convey meanings ranging from the mundane to the political".

Today, we live in a multicultural and diversified world; people, styles and clothes move between one society and another. Yet the idea of Fashion, written with a capital "F", remains inextricably linked to a Western perspective and, according to studies, European and American clothing still enjoys a privileged position today. It is still a commonly held view that Asian, African and Middle Eastern styles fall into the categories of "exotic" or "ethnic".

If we want to say that fashion is an integral part of all human cultures around the world, it would perhaps first be neces-

[4] Dorfles, 2008.

sary to define what fashion is exactly, and herein lies the point: it is industry, history, fabrics, people... it is made of dreams, aspirations, desires, ideals, all elements that are certainly not easy to merge into a single, universally valid definition.

Bloomers, women's puffed trousers, appear towards the end of the 1800s.

Why do we buy?
Novelty, scarcity, hedonism and competition

Fashion is often identified as the industry of consumer materialism par excellence. Defined as frivolous and superficial, it is accused by many of being shaped by the excesses of mass production and unlimited consumption. An industry linked to workers' rights abuses and the indiscriminate pollution of the planet. At the same time, it takes pride of place at the heart of contemporary culture as a sector that offers work and creative opportunities, fostering communication, interpersonal and intercultural relations.

Clothes can be considered a language, a lexicon that speaks as many dialects as there are cultural references [5]. What we wear offers a pretty precise indication of who we are or who we would like to be. Clothing is a language that is as immediate as it is effective, and for many it is the best way to communicate their identity. In the postmodern culture of consumption, products are chosen more for their symbolic properties than for their practical usefulness.

A pair of jeans, shoes or lipstick – once purchased and worn – are part of a process of that create both personal and social identity. In an increasingly material world, mastering dress codes is a nuanced art, influenced by shifting patterns of power, style, authority, play and performance, as well as gender, sex, class, ethnicity and race. From this point of view, shopping takes on a central importance in modern society: buying – as well as being a necessity – has become a need, and the chosen product has the power to transform anyone into the idealised version of themselves.

Contemporary culture is permeated by consumption. Source of happiness for some [6], key point of human existence for others [7]. Since the 1950s, the economy, socio-cultural and psychological transformations have given consumption an increasingly important role in society.

Today, we are overwhelmed with an infinite number of products and services. The process of choice has become imaginary as well as material [8]. Not only do we consume objects, we also consume symbols, shared images that refer to an ideal. To each his own. Whether purchases are

Melanie Pongratz on Unsplash

[5] Lurie, 1981.

[6] Fuat Firat, A., Dholakai, N., "Consuming People: From Political Economy to Theaters of Consumption", *Journal of Consumer Policy 21*, 1998, pp. 339-344.

[7] Hokkanen, S., *Fashion Brands and Consumption in Postmodern Consumer Culture. The Construction of Self and Social Identities*, Swedish School of Textiles, 2014.

The perception of scarcity and the need to create one's own identity lead to purchases.

made at the supermarket, in the village shop, online or at a city boutique, the consumer tries to achieve a certain lifestyle with their choices and shows this to others, expressing their individuality through products.

Clothes and accessories lend themselves well to this by offering the constant possibility of self-improvement, or at least the illusion of it, within reach of the wallet. Building on this concept, the fashion industry has evolved exponentially since the 1980s. Once purely functional, clothes have

[8] Fuat Firat, A., Dholakia, N., Venkatesh, A., "Marketing in a Postmodern World", *European Journal of Marketing*, vol. 29, n. 1, 1995, pp. 40-56.

turned into symbols full of promise, made explicit by increasingly sophisticated advertising images.

Interest in new things is a key pillar of mass consumption, but in the 21st century the meaning of the word "novelty" has taken on epochal connotations. From a small shop in the Spanish city of La Coruña to a global retail empire with over 2,500 shops worldwide, visionary founder of Zara Amancio Ortega has made his brand a global leader in clothing sales. The arrival of the Zara model revolutionised the very idea of fashion: it has transformed the garment into a consumer product and shaken up the canonical seasons along with the modes of production and distribution.

Zara has built a core structure to support the rapid and flexible production of novelty, allowing the Spanish brand to capitalise on trendsetting products that are designed and distributed within a few weeks. In just a couple of decades, "new and fast" have become the watchwords in every retail sector.

The idea inevitably involved everyone in fashion, including the major luxury brands. The thirst for new items has precise scientific explanations. Our brains have evolved to be rewarded by novelty [9], a tendency masterfully exploited by brands and advertising. The preference for all that is new has been preserved in our genetic heritage as an element of evolutionary guarantee; without it, we would not have explored, we would not have been able to find solutions to problems, to create art, to make music, to progress in a constantly changing world.

These dynamics help to explain why we consume even when we don't need to, discarding huge volumes of "things" that are used only temporarily and then replaced, causing enormous damage to the ecosystem. Like a shopping spree in search of a new pair of trousers.

When you walk in, you are excited: there are a thousand choices in the shop, there is a nice smell in the air, a nice atmosphere, everyone is busy browsing, the staff are friendly and helpful. You choose something and try it on, imagining how your colleagues will see you as you walk

[9] Dinnin, A., "The Appeal of Our New Stuff: How Newness Creates Value", *Advances in Consumer Research*, vol. 36, 2009, pp. 261-265.

ZARA BUSINESS MODEL

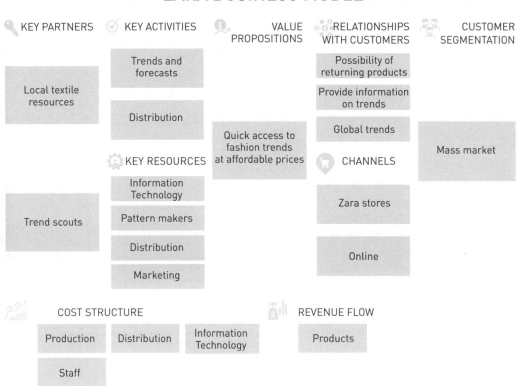

KEY PARTNERS	KEY ACTIVITIES	VALUE PROPOSITIONS	RELATIONSHIPS WITH CUSTOMERS	CUSTOMER SEGMENTATION
Local textile resources	Trends and forecasts		Possibility of returning products	
	Distribution		Provide information on trends	
		Quick access to fashion trends at affordable prices	Global trends	Mass market
	KEY RESOURCES		CHANNELS	
	Information Technology			
Trend scouts	Pattern makers		Zara stores	
	Distribution			
	Marketing		Online	

COST STRUCTURE			REVENUE FLOW
Production	Distribution	Information Technology	Products
Staff			

into the office the next morning and how that apparent piece of cloth will have the power to improve some aspect of your life. The shop may not have the size you need, but that's fine because everything is available 24/7 online. A week after the purchase, the sensations change. The same pair of trousers will have lost its "lustre"; perhaps they don't fall so well, the fabric pinches and the colour is difficult to match. Yet another superfluous spending spree to make us feel guilty, but advertising presses on and the cycle begins again.

From top to bottom, from Gucci to H&M, brands fuel demand by creating limited edition products and sale items at reduced prices – or at least they are perceived as such – in order to create a sense of urgency and to stimulate buyers into opening their wallets again. "Luxury is like a date",

says Guram Gvasalia, former CEO of Vetements: "If something is available in front of you, it is less desirable." The
theory behind contemporary marketing is to meet customer
expectations and needs quickly and effectively in a rapidly
changing world. For products with a shorter life cycle such
as clothing, the speed of market penetration is a key factor
in gaining a competitive advantage. From a psychological
point of view, the urge to buy is mediated by emotions such
as anticipated regret. "It's now or never, or I'll regret it as
soon as I cross the threshold", our brains seem to tell us
as we grapple with a decision to make a purchase that is
somewhat forced by the item's limited availability.

Researchers have found that the perceived scarcity communicated by the retailer somehow threatens the consumer's freedom, triggering immediate and sometimes irra-
tional actions at an unconscious level, such as the purchase
of a pair of shoes that are two sizes too big. Not everyone
responds to stimuli in the same way, but there are certain character traits common to those who would do anything for fashion: competitiveness, hedonism, the need for
uniqueness. Among the sectors that have best been able to
capitalise on "scarcity" is streetwear.

Supreme for Louis Vuitton,
FW 2017.

The American brand Supreme has built an empire on drops, i.e. very limited editions that are available for a specific period of time until sold out – a sales tactic that is used in order to amplify the traditional model of supply and demand.

The cycle typically begins with a social media announcement of an upcoming launch of a limited version of a particular product. Subsequently, the message is amplified through social media, in particular Instagram, where celebrities, fashion influencers and collectors create an echo and the excitement of anticipation mounts. Once products are launched, some may sell out in a matter of seconds, before emerging on resale websites for up to 1,000 times the original price. For brands that have mastered the art of drip sales, the results have been extraordinarily profitable. As with everything in fashion, even the drops – which are often abused – are starting to lose relevance. The customer has learned to recognise and decode the stimuli before the impulse to buy takes over.

The incitement to buy does not only occur through conditioned stimulus-response reflexes. In the digital age, big data – a term which until recently referred exclusively to Silicon Valley tech giants – has now entered the ephemeral world of fashion.

As well as being able to design, produce and distribute a new clothing line in just two weeks, capitalising on a consumer experience centred on impulse purchases, Zara was among the first in fashion to use big data – huge data sets that can be computationally analysed to reveal patterns, trends and associations that are particularly related to human behaviour and interactions – in order to optimise the design and style of its collections according to the trends and needs of its customers.

So, before we call anyone a fashion addict, let's consider how many "tricks" are used – even at an unconscious level – to convince us to buy again and again, despite already having overflowing wardrobes, which play on human weaknesses that are accentuated in a highly competitive and uncertain era.

The fashion industry, which is more global and interconnected than ever, is in the midst of a seismic shift. With the growth of mobile, e-commerce and social media, there is an expectation of speed and convenience when it comes to accessing information, and then there is sustainability to consider, along with a widespread feeling of having reached a limit, even of space in our wardrobes.

Anatomy of a trend

Trends surround us. They are involved in what we eat, what we wear, how we live, they dictate the products and services we want. The oversized or slim jacket. High waist or low waist. Fluo or pastel colours. The trends that define a season usually seem pretty clear, but what we often fail to notice are the interconnections between the key factors that drive them. In fact, fashion does not exist as a phenomenon in itself, it is a reflection of what happens in the world: politics, economics, individual psychology, customs and culture. Trends are the distillation of all of this and represent the *Zeitgeist* of a certain period, they define a spirit, a taste or a mood within a certain social group. The ability to define a set of signs, to frame the evolution of style in order to express what will happen in the future, means revealing the direction of fashions.

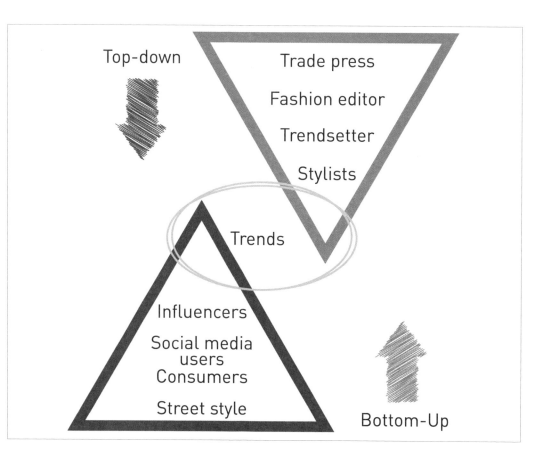

Being able to analyse demand signals is now more important than ever if you are to stay "fashionable"; forecasts of what will work commercially is a crucial issue for successful companies in an environment of demand uncertainty, strong competition, lack of historical data and constant change.

In fashion, the word "trend" represents one of the most enigmatic mysteries of modern culture. In the digital age, the fashion industry's dependence on trend forecasting has radically changed from a symbiotic relationship to a veritable scientific analysis.

In the pre-internet world, the "predictions" were clearly defined. Each link in the supply chain was committed to minimising errors. Identifying a trend was a team effort, developed through consultations between experts in various countries. So-called trendsetters were to be found at fairs and fashion shows, where designers and fashion houses set the agenda of current taste, in city centres, at concerts etc.

Aesthetic sensitivity combined with an ear to the ground on political, social and cultural events would decide which aspects would have the greatest impact on target markets. Details, moods, forecasts of materials, shapes and colours were then outlined in reports or *cahiers de tendances*, which were tailor-made for their respective clients: manufacturers of fibres, fabrics and yarns or large clothing chains and department stores, who would then design collections based on these inputs, would standardise common trends and launch leading proposals.

This was how things worked until the advent of the internet and, later on, social media networks. The general democratisation of information unleashed by the web has overturned many fashion paradigms. The top-down model has been reversed by an intricate web of influencers, from teenagers on YouTube to the weirdest corners of Instagram.

In the last century, fashion trends were initiated by the big fashion houses on a seasonal basis and then disseminated through trade magazines to the final consumer. In the 21st century, novelty has become the engine of commerce, the thirst for new products has spread to every level, and with

the advent of social media, what happens on the street and online has eroded the power of the catwalks. The idea of what constitutes a "trend" has changed today.

In 2019, the largest forecasting company was WGSN, with a market share of 50%. It employs 150 "forecasters" who scour fairs, catwalks, city centres, clubs and concerts in order to discover the next big thing. Their results are then combined with other data, from economic indicators to political sentiment.

It is no longer a question of putting together a few individual aspects, but of extracting a distillation of lifestyles and mentalities, which are then translated into marketable concepts. In *Anatomy of a Trend*, sociologist Henrik Vejlgaard, a pioneer in the field of what is known as trend sociology, argues that there are predictable patterns behind finding the next big thing. Changes in style and taste occur on a regular basis, but the process involved in the birth and evolution of a trend has never been well understood.

Ask anyone what a trend is and the answer will get lost between the vague and the mysterious. According to Vejlgaard, changes don't happen suddenly. "Only human beings can create changes in style and taste. And to the extent that we can understand human beings' behaviour, we can understand how changes in style and taste come about."

After analysing past trends in several categories, including clothing, the Danish sociologist identified nine conditions which, if met, would give rise to a new trend. "The next big thing", in commercial terms, always begins as a reaction to what is in the mainstream. Several trendsetters then adopt the trend, followed by a gradually increasing number of other people. Cities are almost always the birthplace of new trends: the most culturally and economically lively city centres popularise new habits; it is important that styles and products can be imitated or copied.

And then of course we must look at the media on which the trend resonates. The connection between popularity (primarily films and music), and the diffusion of new styles or reinterpreted styles, is key. Trends start out as simple ideas that are adopted by key players in the fashion world and then make their way to the general public, before coming to prominence. Trends that become very popular very suddenly tend to disappear over time, once they are adopted by the mainstream. They therefore have a chance of being recycled and serve as inspiration again in the future.

In the internet age, if you want to look at the popularity of a certain topic or product, Google is an excellent starting point. In 2013, Ozweego trainers – a bulky pair of Adidas trainers designed by Raf Simons and inspired by the famous vintage Adidas, New Balance and Sketchers designs of the 90s and reinterpreted with new colours and fabrics – caught the attention of fashion followers and sneakerheads on the hunt for something new. In the following seasons, the trend appeared at Balenciaga, Dior Homme, Gucci, Lanvin, Prada and Acne Studios, each with their own version designed for male consumers seduced by streetwear.

The launch of designer Demna Gvasalia's signature Balenciaga Triple S in January 2017 marked the turning point. Initially worn more for fun, the shoe has become the symbol of the emerging ugly shoes trend. The hype was turned into sales and the Triple S – retailing for over €650 – sold out within seconds of going on sale, both on the shelf and online.

A year after the launch, the Triple S was still a bestseller, with retailers struggling to maintain stock. Two years later, the trend was in its death throes: thousands of versions,

Top left: Adidas Ozweego trainers.
Top right: Balenciaga Triple S.
Below: Dior B22.

recycled and updated, had filtered down to every level of the market, from luxury to low cost.

As well as an interest in all things '90s, the explosion of sportswear and streetwear styles played a huge role, and their bold features made them ideal for posting on Instagram. Emphasising the need to be as attuned as possible to consumer demands, and developing their flexibility in order to respond to changing trends, companies that reacted quickly were able to capitalise on this.

In his bestseller, *The Tipping Point*, Malcolm Gladwell offers an interesting analysis of how trends work. As Gladwell recounts, the Hush Puppies shoe company was a dying brand in late 1994 until some New York hipsters made it fashionable again.

After that the cool kids copied the fashion, other fashionistas followed suit, and so on, until, *voilà!* Within two years, Hush Puppies' sales had exploded by a staggering 5,000% without a dollar spent on advertising.

All because, as Gladwell says, a small number of super influential characters (twenty, fifty, a hundred at most) started wearing the shoes.

These were not celebrities like Kim Kardashian, but ordinary people with flair who were able to catalyse trends. This was actually a rather old marketing concept that dates back to 1955, when pioneering sociologists Elihu Katz and Paul F. Lazarsfeld wrote the book, *Personal Influence*.

They assert that advertising has influenced society through a two-step process: companies convey messages, which are then adopted by opinion leaders, who proselytise and set trends. Reach out to those opinion leaders, Katz and Lazarsfeld argued, and you'll quickly convert the masses.

Today, fashion houses and designers still have an impact on the way trends emerge, but they no longer hold the monopoly. Fashion trends now start and evolve through other key channels: besides the catwalk, there is the street, there are celebrities, Instagram influencers.

Having returned to the front pages after years of oblivion, it is haute couture these days, rather than prêt-à-porter (which is often more sensitive to market demands) that creates culture and gives a brand its status. This is the theatre of excellence, extravagance and experimentation as an end in itself, a high celebration of fashion – for the very few of course – but whose reflection can still be compared to the trickle down model sanctioned by Veblen. From here comes the ideal, that of beauty and fashion being disconnected from function, the pure dream, and from there comes input and suggestions that are then cascaded into the increasingly crowded world of fashion.

Despite hundreds of studies, there is still little evidence to support economist George Taylor's theory that skirt hems lengthen during periods of economic growth, or Leonard Lauder's suggestion that lipstick sales increase during a recession.

To cope with ever-changing technologies, market analysts and marketers are rapidly evolving, moving away from traditional static criteria based on demographics, to more dynamic, modern influences linked to mood, lifestyle, psycho-graphic and of course technological surveys.

Technology has given marketers precious data that is mostly left by our virtual footprints: consumption habits, online purchases, app searches, leisure preferences, etc., which if

Sportswear, Tommy Hilfiger,
SS 18.

read correctly, at least on a theoretical level, would guarantee infallible forecasts.

Traditional forecasting is threatened by data-driven analytics. The clothing industry's supply chain is becoming increasingly digital and flexible, while Google also has a trendspotting section that releases a regular fashion trends report at the end of the year, based on the company's vast array of research data. The results are still basic: in 2019, searches for '90s fashion was on the rise, while many people had lost interest in the '60s, in terms of style. The aim

is to produce more sophisticated combinations of search and data combinations. Whether artificial intelligence will ever truly replace traditional fashion forecasting methods remains to be seen.

Some fear that the excessive use of artificial intelligence can make design monotonous. For others, the ingenuity of imaginative couturiers will prevail over the homogeneity of data-based algorithms.

Status and aspirations. Logos and meanings

We live in the era of the brand. Emblems, usually based on the name or initials of a company, imprinted or applied to objects to distinguish and recognise them by, can now be seen everywhere. Overt or covert, brands and logos have a lot to say. A logo does not only serve to identify a product, its presence is the visual representation of a company's identity.

The historical perspective of brands evolves "from an emphasis on ownership to an emphasis on a product's quality and its origins" [10]. As far back as 2000 BC, we start to see the first evidence of branding as a procedure for identifying the ownership and origin of goods. This would be seen on livestock as well as Chinese ceramic articles, Indian objects, Greek pottery and Roman bricks and tiles.

The logo does not only serve to identify a product, its popularity is closely linked to the concept of quality assurance. In 12th century England, producers of bread, gold and silver goods were required to print unique symbols on their produce to ensure the honesty of weights and measures.

The modern logo is equivalent to the trademark used by manufacturers in the mediaeval era, i.e. a guarantee of authenticity, a pictorial device of central importance in the ever-changing world of fashion. An effective logo creates brand loyalty and gives status to those who wear it. Among the most successful historical ones, the Nike logo – an abstract visual symbol called the Swoosh, created in 1971 – has gone down in history as one of the most incisive and recognisable logos ever.

In fashion, image is everything and it is in this sector that the logo takes on crucial importance. Styles and trends change constantly, but a successful logo is rarely altered. When that does happen, they are subtle rather than radical aesthetic changes.

Fashion's most iconic logos are also the most versatile: Chanel's double "C" (introduced by Karl Lagerfeld in 1983) or Louis Vuitton's age-old "LV" letters, are well suited to

[10] Yang, D., Sonmez, M., Li, Q. (2012), "Marks and Brands: Conceptual, Operational and Methodological Comparisons, *Journal of Intellectual Property Rights*, vol. 17, pp. 315-323. Briciu V., Briciu A., "A Brief History of Brands and The Evolution of Place Branding", *Bulletin of the Transilvania University of Brasov*, Series VII: Social Sciences and Law, vol. 9 (58), 2016. Moore and Reid, 2008, p. 6.

clasps or buckles, but also work equally well translated into patterns on fabrics or embossed on leather and other materials.

Versace's Medusa head picks up on a classic architectural motif that is perfect for printing on objects and accessories – not only on clothing, but also on cosmetics and household products, both textile and ceramic.

A highly recognisable logo can be a company's greatest financial asset. Such is its importance that trademark protection has become an international legal discipline.

Shape, colour, graphics – every detail in the global market can be easily copied and counterfeited, causing hundreds of millions of dollars of damage to the companies that own them. The body of law governing trademark protection came into being in the mid-19th century in Europe and the United States. Despite being constantly violated, it has spread to countries such as India and China.

In history, the use of the logo as a decorative element can be said to have been the exclusive preserve of the luxury industry. Leather goods manufacturers were the first to fully exploit its potential.

In 1896, Frenchman Louis Vuitton first used its monogram in the form of a pattern on trunks and travel bags. At the time, these items were intended exclusively for wealthy customers, the only ones able to afford long and comfortable first-class journeys aboard ships or trains. Since then, the PVC-coated cotton canvas luggage branded with the letters "LV" has remained the company's staple.

The same can be said for Gucci, whose double "G" – which has been reinterpreted several times throughout its history – was adopted from the 1960s onwards. The turning point in the development of fashion branding came with the signature or logo being moved from the inside of the garment or accessory to the outside. In the second half of the 19th century, the most famous designers (starting with the first couturier in the modern sense, Charles Frederick Worth) began to sew small labels with their names printed on them inside their clothes.

Above: Louis Vuitton, SS 18.
Below: Chanel, FW 2020.

Versace Home, 2016.

In the beginning, the main concern was to avoid the circulation of fakes. It would be in the area of sportswear that the logo would rise to prominence. In 1940, the Fred Perry brand – named after the tennis star of the same name – borrowed an idea from contemporary sports clubs, that of displaying their logo on the chest.

In the 1970s, when sportswear left the playing fields and moved into leisurewear, other brands like Lacoste followed suit, paving the way for the sportswear greats and making the phenomenon explode globally by the end of the last century.

The 1980s definitively cleared the way for brand logos to be on display. Thanks to street culture, which has been in the spotlight ever since, what became known as the "designer decade" would sanction the company's lasting success in the mass market. Rappers, for example, would make their way into the fashion imagination. With their arrival come heavy gold necklaces featuring metal Mercedes and BMW logos as pendants – symbols of status, style and spending power.

This trend was taken to the extreme by sportswear brands such as Nike and Tommy Hilfiger, and was revived at the end of the century by the world's biggest fashion brands.

Gucci, Dior, Fendi and Vuitton all followed the trend of exhibiting the brand, creating collections based entirely on logo patterns.

The first and most obvious side effect was the proliferation of the counterfeit industry. In an industry that relied more on a simple signature than on the intrinsic quality of its products, counterfeiting became the easiest way to make money off a brand by exploiting its name.

As always happens, excess produces its opposite: the wave of brands caused a cultural and political reaction of rejection following the success of Naomi Klein's book *No Logo*, which was published in 1999 as the anthem of the anti-globalisation movement and the denunciation of brand capitalism. Brazenly branded products were accused of labour exploitation, a symbol of social inequality and oppressive late capitalism.

In fashion, everything is repeated and in the second decade of the 2000s – after a few years of oblivion – logos returned, even more charged with meaning. Again thanks to street culture, the logo took on the reputation of the company it represents. No longer so much a question of conveying messages of power, it is more about a specific lifestyle that is associated with it.

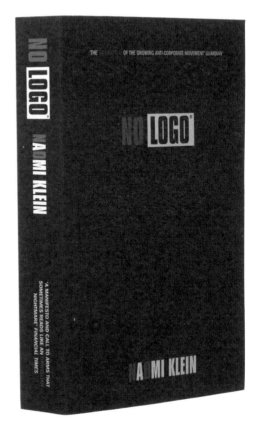

BALMAIN
PARIS

BALMAIN
PARIS

Above: Balmani logo restyling.
Below: Versace logo restyling.

Today, in a saturated market, a successful logo must embody the corporate identity. Visual information accounts for 90% of brain input, an image is processed 60,000 times faster than text – a major communication advantage that the biggest fashion brands have certainly not missed. The most recognisable logos are treated like human faces. We see hundreds of them every day but only a few are familiar to us, we connect with them and by recognising them we engage in listening to what they have to say.

As in human interaction, they evoke feelings and effects that are quite memorable. Logos are the most powerful marketing tool that companies have at their disposal, they reflect values and principles which, if conveyed well, translate into sales.

How does this process happen? In this case, psychology offers a number of possible answers. "It is impossible to wear clothes without transmitting social signals; each garment tells a story, often a very subtle one about the wearer." [11]

[11] Morris, D., 1977.

[12] Davis, L. L., Lennon, S. J., "Social Cognition And The Study Of Clothing And Human Behavior. Social Behavior and Personality", *International Journal*, n. 16, 1988, pp. 175-186.

The field of social psychology boasts extensive literature on the perception of people based on first impressions [12].

Clothing, it has been pointed out, is a fundamental characteristic that is used by the human brain to formulate an initial opinion about someone.

1980-1990

GIANNI VERSACE

1990-1997

1993-1997

1997-2008

VERSACE

2008-....

In the film *Pretty Woman*, Julia Roberts' character Vivian is rudely kicked out of a Sunset Boulevard boutique for wearing a skimpy dress and heavy make-up. "You're obviously in the wrong place. Please go away", the unfriendly shop assistants tell her. In a later scene, Vivian returns to the same boutique, laden with designer bags and wearing expensive clothes – the sales assistants receive her quite differently.

Research confirms this dynamic: one's wardrobe is very important. We treat people differently based on their clothing. In a 2011 study, psychologists Nelissen and Meijers highlight the social benefits of luxury brands as signals of status and wealth: the display and consumption of luxury goods would cause favourable treatment in social interactions. In

the study *The Rival Wears Prada* [13] it was found that, among women, the consumption of luxury brands would be used to compete with peers. In relationships with other women, however, those who wore luxury items were considered to be younger, more ambitious, sexier and more attractive, but also less loyal, of lower intelligence and immature. In short, do the benefits outweigh the costs?

Fashion evolves and so does branding. In recent years, so-called "luxury" brands seem largely oriented towards cleanliness of form and font legibility. This is a practical choice that makes brands more suitable for online distribution; a font's elegance and clarity also gives it versatility, allowing brands to change course while remaining consistent with fluctuating market trends.

[13] Hudders, L., Department of Communication Sciences, Ghent University, 2014.

THE LURE OF LUXURY

Luxury: from vice to marketing tool

"Display of wealth, pomp, magnificence; a tendency (even habitual, as a standard of living) for superfluous, uncontrolled expenditure, for the purchase and use of objects which, either because of their quality or ornamentation, have no use corresponding to their price, and are intended to satisfy ambition and vanity more than an actual need". According to the Treccani encyclopedia, this is the modern definition of luxury, but throughout history, its meaning – the notion, the metaphor and the word itself – has undergone a radical transformation, from a generic vice to a powerful marketing tool.

Hermès Birkin bag, Nile Crocodile version in albino crocodile skin and diamonds.

Alligator bags with diamond decorations that cost the same as a city apartment, fifteen-course meals eaten with pure gold cutlery, yachts the length of a city block; our discomfort with excess is nothing new.

Even the ancient Greeks and Romans were concerned with finding the delicate balance between luxury and morality. The reputation of luxury as a metaphor for vice or sin (the opposite of virtue), arose from the belief that it was the cause and symptom of social disorder. Luxury as a moral issue becomes central to Christian theology, its presence signaling the danger of subversion of simple human needs. Corruption and greed not only threatened the moral well-being of the individual, but could also poison the body politic and lead to the collapse of the entire society. In short, indulging in luxury was a grave sin [1].

Around 215 BC, Roman senators first started to enact laws to control the way people could dress and entertain themselves. Sumptuary laws, so named because they related to

[1] Riello, McNeil, 2016.

Ambrogio Lorenzetti, *The Allegory of Good and Bad Government* (detail), 1338, Palazzo Pubblico, Siena.

personal expenditure, aimed to curb the excesses associated with the display of superfluity and wealth.

The *Lex Oppia*, among the first to be enacted by the Roman Senate in 215 BC, stipulated that women could not wear more than half a gram of gold in jewellery and ornaments, and that their tunics should not be of different colours. Over the centuries, many other such laws followed.

In 1300, when national governments were established in France and England, and city-states were formed in Italy, sumptuary laws appeared throughout Europe. Florence in 1322 forbade its citizens to wear clothes made from scarlet silk outside their homes. In 1366, Perugia forbade the wearing of velvet, silk and satin within its borders. In

England in 1337, Edward III decreed that no one below the rank of knight could wear fur.

In the 17th century, such laws were mostly used to limit imports from abroad. France, for example, established its own silk industry and banned English silks and textiles, using the excuse that they were too luxurious. Italy and Spain, however, continued to impose class restrictions on clothing until the 1800s.

The concept of fashion as we understand it today has only existed since the 17th century. The term derives from the French *à la mode*, whose Latin root *modus* (meaning way of being and measuring) scholars say first appeared in 1482 to refer to specific styles of clothing. About seventy years later, people would talk about "following fashions" and "new fashion".

Fashion as a modern social phenomenon was born out of industrialisation, commercialisation and the democratisation of consumption and luxury. In this context, a radical change takes place in the perception of the latter: from a generic sin to a marketing tool for the new rising capitalism.

With the help of popular culture – not least the Hollywood film industry – luxury is celebrated through consumption: decriminalised and cleansed of the burden of sin, it becomes a means of gaining status and social respect. Rather than being a phenomenon that is the exclusive prerogative of the wealthy classes, it becomes something to aspire to, a concept connected to taste, fashion, social and economic competition, a positive trade force.

In the 18th century, what would become the key concepts of "modern luxury" are established: luxury goods are no longer necessarily made of precious materials, their intrinsic value is separated from an economic one. The prestige and reputation of the manufacturer, or the brand, is of fundamental importance in attributing the value of a product.

From 1760 onwards, a series of publications dedicated to women's fashions appear on the market. Advertising becomes an integral part and the engine of the new consumer culture.

Scene from *Breakfast at Tiffany's*, a film that exploded the obsession with the little black dress.

In Western countries over the centuries, there has been a fundamental ideological change with regard to what is considered to be superfluous spending. That is, the "ideological neutralisation of consumption [...] which frees itself from the persistent suspicion of waste, social injustice and materialism that have always opposed it". [2]

The following centuries would see luxury goods gradually turn into conventional signs, symbols of a new hierarchy of relationships between people and things.

The new millennium would see luxury spending pass from objects to experiences to personal transformation, where an improved version of oneself becomes the product. Its very definition has been dramatically expanded and diluted. For some, it means fine wines, penthouses, exclusive

[2] Fabris, Minestroni, 2004, p. 65.

clubs and designer clothes. For others, it might be dining at a restaurant, a much-dreamed-of holiday or something as simple as settling down on the sofa with a good book.

Although the phenomenon of luxury has existed since ancient times, [3] it is only recently that the industry associated with it has grown at a spectacular rate [4].

There are a number of reasons for the exponential increase in the consumption of luxury goods, including the continued growth of economic wealth in developed countries, the rise of the middle class and its level of income and, more recently, the incredible economic development of so-called "emerging countries", with China in the lead [5].

In the 21st century, luxury is no longer a restricted sector aimed only at the lucky few with pockets full of cash. Luxury products and brands are now ubiquitous, tangible signs of globalisation and the consumer society.

The magic of marketing.
I don't need it but I do

In the course of the 14th century, hand in hand with industrialisation, the spread of wealth, printing and advertising, the quantity of products available on the market increased exponentially. Cities become the scene of commerce, and competition becomes a hot topic among retailers looking for customers.

An early version of marketing is seen in the form of what became known as trade cards, or printed flyers delivered by shopkeepers directly into the hands of potential customers. Today this is commonplace, but in the 1800s it was considered the final frontier in the field of promotion.

The variety of trade cards was immense: from grocery stores owners to wholesalers, from hairdressers to shoemakers and hatters – every major trader invested in their image through visually appealing messages. Unlike advertisements that seek to persuade an anonymous audience to consume particular goods and services, trade cards were

[3] Godey, B., Pederzoli, D., Aiello, G., Donvito, R., Wiedmann, K. P., Hennigs, N., "A Cross-cultural Exploratory Content Analysis of the Perception of Luxury from Six Countries", *Journal of Product and Brand Management*, n. 22, 2013, pp. 229-237.

[4] Hennigs, N., Wiedmann, K. P., Behrens, S., Klarmann, C., "Unleashing the Power of luxury: Antecedents of Luxury Brand Perception and Effects on Luxury Brand Strength, *Journal of Brand Management*, n. 20, 2013, pp. 705-715.

[5] Cavender, R., Kincade, D., "Management of a Luxury Brand: Dimensions and Sub-variables from a Case Study of LVMH", *Journal of Fashion Marketing and Management*, n.18, 2014.

A printer's trade card, England, 17th century.

Trade card belonging to Thomas Smith and his Indian Queen fabric shop.

⁶ Riello, 2012, p. 103.

freely distributed among a known or anticipated customer base as a reminder of a business location or specialisation.

One of the many that is remembered is that of Thomas Smith of London, a seller of textiles whose shop opened under the sign "Indian Queen", accompanied by the image of an Indian queen escorted by an assistant holding a delicate parasol above her head. The association and allure of the exotic was intended to attract a clientele in search of exclusive and sophisticated merchandise. And so marketing was born ⁶.

The idea of what is considered luxury changes radically throughout eras and cultures: from the 20th century onwards, it would no longer be the price that gives a product its value. At the risk of oversimplification, what defines a person in society is a combination of what they do and what they have.

Yet many companies would have us believe that who we are depends solely on what we buy. Once upon a time, luxury was synonymous with quality. The most famous fashion brands have built their reputations on the best materials and the most skilled craftsmen, charging customers extra for both.

But at some point, things got complicated. Perception and desirability play an important role in the pricing game. The higher the price, the more exclusive and desirable the item becomes.

And then there is perceived scarcity, the impression that is promoted by the industry whereby its products are desirable because they are rare and exclusive, destined only for the lucky few. In reality or perception, demand is always disproportionate to supply; the marketing executive maintains this balance like the magician uses a magic wand. It is surprising that almost the entire luxury industry is based on this fundamental principle, despite producing bags, clothes and a myriad of other goods for the mass market.

In reality, modern luxury brands have perfected the art of selling exclusivity in millions of units, with the aim of satisfying the human desire to belong to a group and, at the same time, stand out from the crowd.

There remain, of course, examples of excellence, where scarcity actually does equal exclusivity: the movement for a Bulgari Magsonic Sonnerie Tourbillon contains over 900 hand-finished parts – the time required to put together a complicated watch in this category can easily exceed two years. Not surprisingly, the price is high enough to return substantial profit margins, and demand that exceeds supply only increases the value.

Scarcity is also celebrated in retail. Making distribution exclusive and selective allows you to control the experience: limit the time products are available for with exclusive previews and long waiting lists. These mechanisms aim to fuel desirability. A high price point is the most obvious signal, but when all elements are well calibrated, price is no longer demand's driving force.

Brand communication is the most powerful weapon for a well-trained expert tasked with fuelling a dream, creating desire. In postmodern consumer culture, products are bought and used for their symbolic value. The act of possessing and exhibiting has become so important that the chosen objects have become an extension of the Self, a means of differentiation between individuals and groups of people.

A version of the Bulgari Magsonic.

Numerous studies in the field of psychology have found that the consumption of fashion brands plays a particularly important role in the construction of an adult's identity. By choosing a particular brand, we communicate personality, identity and social relationships.

Since the beginning of the new millennium, the price of luxury fashion products has grown exponentially. Whereas in 2000, you "only" needed around €4,500 to take home a Hermès Kelly bag, in 2020 you would need more than twice that amount. This kind of price increase may seem dispro-portionate, especially when compared to the European and the United States' consumer price index, but in recent years two new factors have entered the equation.

The economic development of powers such as China has opened the door to the lucrative category of the so-called *nouveau riche* (those who aim to immediately communicate their newly-attained social status through the purchase of conspicuously expensive items). This was the case with the economic rise of Japan and the United States in the last century and the Chinese boom today. It is no coincidence that China accounted for 35% of the entire luxury market in 2019.

With economic development comes social mobility; rising wages for the working class also provides an opportunity to indulge in the purchase of luxury goods, an activity from which they were previously precluded. There's nothing new about this. But in the age of social media, selfie culture has made what was previously private accessible to everyone in the entire world. With millions of people posting "better versions" of themselves every day, the human desire to stand out has never been more intense. Visibility offered by social media – Instagram in particular – has exponentially increased the number of people looking for ways to stand out, through the conspicuous display of expensive goods, among other things.

BEYOND THE PRODUCT

In the 21st century, luxury spending has shifted from objects to experiences, a trend linked to the rise of the so-called "experience economy" theorised by B. Joseph Pine II and James H. Gilmore in their book of the same name written back in 1999, but which contains very contemporary ideas.

The book gives the example of the humble cup of coffee. Coffee is a crucial metaphor of Pine and Gilmore's theory, a theory that concretizes the message "goods and services are no longer enough". As a consumer commodity, coffee beans cost a few cents per cup. Ground, packaged and sold in the supermarket, the branded coffee is sold for five to eight cents a cup. At the bar, as part of a service, those same beans cost one euro per cup. Add a little atmosphere in a downtown coffee shop to the water and ground powder and the price of that cup of coffee goes up to three euros. Order an espresso at Caffè Florian in Piazza San Marco in Venice and the cost of that memorable experience exceeds eight euros.

Above: Hermès Kelly bag.
Below: Grace Kelly, the actress-princess who inspired it.

[7] Silverstein, M., Fiske, N., 2004.

The basic idea is that today experience represents a previously undefined "genre of economic production". An evolved type of offer, beyond commodities, goods and services. When you buy a product, you are buying a series of intangible qualities that are related to it. But when you buy an experience, you are spending money on enjoying a series of memorable events that a company stages like a theatrical performance, in an attempt to engage you on a personal level.

In this context, in the new millennium, the consumption of luxury is driven by four basic motivations or "emotional spaces" [7]: the need to take care of oneself, to pamper oneself, which stems from the belief that personal gratification is, in this difficult world, an acquired right. The desire to establish and cultivate relationships, however, varies with age. For a single person, the purchase of a very expensive garment can play a central role in the search for a partner as a sign of good taste, culture and professional success.

Interior of the Caffè Florian, Venice.

In recent years, shopping has also taken on new connotations; it is now more akin to research, an exploration, a way of obtaining new and intellectual stimuli. Finally, the last motivation is linked to the desire to express one's taste through specific style choices.

So far nothing new, except that in the new millennium the consumer is not looking for a brand or an object to signal their wealth according to the logic of the status symbol. Today's buyers of luxury products look for brands that are consistent with their values and personal style.

What they want to highlight is their ability to appreciate some peculiar characteristics of the product, which is a particularly valid reason in the field of fashion [8]. In this sense, it is clear that the traditional idea of luxury goods as simply expensive objects has been superseded in favour of a new concept of emotion-based spending. It is precisely on these emotions that modern marketing leverages.

By nature, human beings are preoccupied with metaphysics and seek transcendence.

In addition to products and services, companies – especially those in the luxury bracket – also sell myths and communicate values as well as other intangible assets. These meta-assets, e.g. prestige, beauty, strength and success, are the main strengths in the context of contemporary market-

[8] Fabris, 2003.

ing. Fashion advertising campaigns draw heavily from the well of human values and feelings, which are deeply rooted in ideals, desires, and symbols of social recognition.

The art of selling dreams
Economic and emotional value

In the Middle Ages, sumptuary laws specified in great detail what was appropriate and what was forbidden for each social class. Among the many things it laid out was the maximum sales price permitted for clothing and accessories. The idea behind it was that certain fabrics and ornaments would be reserved for certain classes so that a distinction would be made between each, allowing order within the social hierarchy to be maintained.

A special case in point was the extravagant wardrobe of Queen Elizabeth I (1533-1603), which was designed and created as visual proof of her "divine" status. During the 18th century, the industrial revolution and the development of trade as a vehicle of social mobility led to the rise of the bourgeoisie and cities replacing courts, marking the end of the sumptuary laws. However, the consumption and use of personal goods as symbols of status has remained a constant for centuries [9].

In 1899, economist Thorstein Veblen observed that silver spoons and corsets had become true markers of social standing for the elite. In his very famous treatise *The Theory of the Leisure Class*, Veblen coined the term "conspicuous consumption" to refer to the way in which material objects were bought and flaunted as proof of economic power.

More than a hundred years later, conspicuous consumption is still part of the contemporary social landscape, yet luxury goods are significantly more accessible today than in Veblen's day. "Accessible" luxury is a feature of the 20th century's mass production economy, of globalisation, of outsourcing production to developing countries, where labour and raw materials are cheaper. At the same time, the rise of the middle class has led to a higher demand for material goods at more affordable prices.

[9] Berry, 1994, p. 82.

The democratisation of consumer goods has made them less effective as signals of status. Faced with growing social inequality, both the rich and those we could define as "comfortable" can afford the latest generation of smartphones and designer handbags.

Both groups own SUVs, take planes, go on cruises and shop on Net-a-Porter. On the surface, these two groups' favourite consumer objects no longer reside in two completely different universes.

Designer handbags and new cars are no longer the exclusive prerogative of the elite; in a world overrun with commodities of all kinds, social distinctions have gradually become more subtle. Yachts, Bentleys and pure gold fittings still exist, but in the 21st century the new style frontier is played out on the field of experience and culture.

The new educated and affluent elite consolidate their status through the construction of cultural capital, and spending habits that arise from this [10]. The new "aspirational class" prefers to spend money on services, education and experiences, rather than on purely material goods: dinner in a 5-star restaurant, organic groceries, a planned trip to the opening of an exhibition, a prestigious university for the children. This style of consumption is inconspicuous but extremely expensive, showing itself through less obvious but equally significant signals.

Hand in hand with this, the democratisation of luxury has paved the way for a flood of products that are accessible to many, despite being expensive. There was a time when the meaning of luxury was part aspiration, part exclusivity and part signalling something whose price was so high as to be beyond the reach of most mere mortals. It was the Hermès bag, the Cartier watch or the pure cashmere designer coat that signaled status and exuded wealth. Brands communicated through magazines.

An arbiter of aesthetic refinement, the printed word had the power to fascinate readers and consumers. Those were the days in which craftsmanship, rarity, exclusive design and high-quality materials constituted the DNA of every luxury product worthy of the name. But times have changed;

[10] Currid-Halkett, 2017.

Elizabeth I in *An Allegory of The Tudor Succession* (detail), attributed to Lucas de Heere, 1572. National Museum Cardiff.

brands and magazines have lost their monopoly on image control.

Today, everyone can have their say by communicating tastes, preferences, stories and thoughts on social media. In recent years, the market has been flooded with items that are advertised as being exclusive despite being inherently banal. These are rather ordinary designer items, often with large logos in plain view, such as trainers, tracksuits and rubber slippers, which are considered luxury products by virtue of a tag.

Research from the California Institute of Technology investigated how the cost of a product affects the perception of quality [11]. The results show that price is crucial for value recognition: the data suggests that people assume that more expensive items are superior or more effective than less expensive options, even when they have the same quality and features. This conclusion alone is not enough to justify a three-figure price for a simple pair of tennis shoes, even if they are designer.

[11] Zeithaml, V., "Consumer Perceptions of Price, Quality, and Value: A Means-End Model and Synthesis of Evidence", *Journal of Marketing*, vol. 52, n. 3, 1988, pp. 2-22.

So why do consumers buy so-called luxury products at prices that are often difficult to justify? Several studies show that their appeal is mainly psychological, so it is the emotions associated with the judgements that guide us in making purchasing decisions. According to researchers, the decision to buy a designer product is inextricably linked to the emotional sphere. Consequently, purchasing behaviour is a direct result of how a consumer perceives a brand, along with how that brand's product is able to deliver the emotional benefits associated with owning it. In this process, the final emotional benefit affects the concept of Self: the choice of a high-end product is therefore driven by evaluations of personal identity, ideal Self and social comparison.

It involves a mix of emotions in which self-esteem, hedonism, satisfaction and perceived power become the driving force and impetus to make a purchase.

A second degree of involvement was found in affluent consumers, who are therefore used to choosing high-end designer products.

For them, trust, security and fulfilment are the predominant feelings linked to the perception that the brands they choose are authentic and timeless. Beyond the design, workmanship and materials used, what matters to this consumer group is the rare and intangible quality of truth. "While this truth derives from a product's design and features, it is primarily determined by a deeper understanding of the brand's essence. Truth is expressed in the narrative and images that bring the brand to life, evoking perceptions of timeless authenticity."

A front row seat: diffusion of fashions between tradition and innovation

Man has been wearing clothes for centuries, but when did the fashion dream begin? The "fashion system", i.e. the broad social and cultural phenomenon that encompasses not only business but also creativity, craftsmanship, production, consumption and communication, is a product of Western civilisation.

At the end of the 14th century, fashion was still a very limited phenomenon within individual courts. By the end of the 16th century, however, fashion became an indicator of widespread class status, and was monopolised by a luxury-obsessed aristocracy. As early as 1600, the lower classes were trying to climb the social ladder by adopting the clothing of the upper classes: this is how fashion came out of the palaces, becoming a topic of interest for an increasing number of men and women.

It was in this context that the industry's first experiments in communication began, with information on the styles in vogue being disseminated from one country to another on the European continent. Fashion plates – drawings, engravings or illustrations depicting clothes, shoes, hairstyles and accessories – first came into circulation in England and France in the late 16th century and quickly spread throughout Western Europe.

Arbiters of aesthetic taste, these illustrations can be considered the ancestors of modern fashion magazines, where clothes and details were key considerations. Printing processes advanced rapidly in the 19th century, a time when the systems that are still used today were first introduced. This allowed runs to be made at a low cost, meaning publications could be made available to a wide audience.

GIORNALE DELLE FAMIGLIE
Mode de Paris
Milano Via Pietro Verri 12.
1 Ottobre 1867

Fashion plates, 1836-1867.

The printing of books, newspapers and magazines is still of importance today, not only in the dissemination of culture but also in terms of social and civic education. The mechanisation of printing operations in 1812 gave an unprecedented boost to the dissemination of trends, and from then until just a few years ago, newspapers and magazines were the preferred place to communicate fashion.

REVUE DE LA MODE

Fashion plates, 1883.

French newspaper *Mercure Galant* was the first publication in history to dedicate a special edition entirely to the subject. From 1672 onwards, clothes, shoes and accessories became something to talk about. Donneau de Visé, founder of *Mercure Galant*, was the first journalist to take an interest in concepts that are now the basis of fashion discourse. He is credited with introducing the idea of the season, and his special edition with the eloquent title *Extraordinaire* boasted a second brilliant insight, namely his target audience, women. Before then, no publication, neither printed nor engraved, had aimed to intercept tastes peculiar to the female audience.

Left: *Mercure Galant*, 1679.
Right: François Gérard, *Louis XVIII of France in Coronation Robes*, 1782-1837.

Despite substantial geographical variables, colourful, co-quettish fashion, adorned with bows, lace and intricate embroidery was the prerogative of the man of the court, particularly the French court, and would remain so until the beginning of the 19th century when the ideals of bourgeois respectability would prevail.

Monsieur de Visé's moves, audacious at the time, are considered by historians to be ingenious marketing techniques that propelled a fledgling industry into the mainstream. From then until the end of the 20th century, the trade press would be the privileged showcase for fashion, the communication tool of choice, the *trait d'union* between designers, industry and consumers, the only one capable of catalysing expectations, dreams and desires.

In Italy, the first periodicals to be specifically aimed at women appeared in Florence around 1770 and were committed to providing advice and suggestions to ladies, young wives

Moda di Francia   Moda di Parigi   Moda di Francia

Some pages from the *Corriere delle dame*, 1819-1835-1824.

and sensible daughters. They aimed to educate while they delighted the reader, as evidenced by the titles: *La Toelette, Biblioteca galante, Giornale delle dame*. The Florentine periodicals were followed by those published in Milan, the *Corriere delle dame e delle mode di Francia*, and those published in Venice, such as *La donna galante ed erudita*.

But fashion wasn't just a female topic. Some fashion magazines, such as *Gentleman's Magazine of Fashions, Fancy Costumes, The Regimentals of the Army and Splendidly Embellished* were aimed at a male audience. This was an indicative fact that underlined the impact of fashion on culture as a whole, not just on a particular gender.

Throughout the 19th century, women's magazines were profitable businesses that demonstrated sharp growth. Some of these specialised magazines talked about cooking, furniture and embroidery, while many focused on fashion.

In the early 1900s, women's fashion magazines took another leap into the future, moving from illustrations to photographs and ushering in an era of excess, which was reflected in the glossy pages of the most popular fashion magazines.

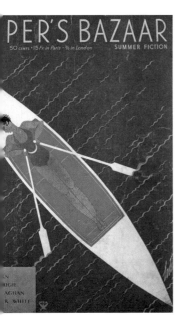

Until the 1940s and 1950s, however, fashion journalism was limited to a dry reporting of styles and details, such as lengths of dresses and skirts, cuts and fabrics. It was thanks to magazines such as *Vogue* and *Harper's Bazaar*, founded in 1892 and 1867 respectively, that a creative and colourful style of writing made its appearance in the glossy pages of the major fashion industry periodicals.

In 1962, Diana Vreeland moved from *Harper's Bazaar* to *Vogue America* as associate editor. In 1963, Sam Newhouse, owner of Condé Nast, promoted her to editor-in-chief in an attempt to reinvigorate the publication. Having gained complete control over layout and content, Diana would mark the turning point not only for *Vogue*, but for the entire universe of fashion magazines, thanks to her original style and taste for the fantastical.

Harper's Bazaar, July 1934.

Left: Twiggy on the cover of *Vogue*, 1967.
Right: *Vogue*, 1962.

During Vreeland's reign, the magazine's editorial circulation presented a dream of exoticism and aristocratic glamour to the general public and – last but not least – it fixed the stereotype of the contemporary model (which was so atypical for the time) in the common imagination. Veruschka, Penelope Tree, Twiggy and Lauren Hutton all appeared to

be very young, each with a strong look and slim bodies with unisex appeal. Just as clothing has the ability to transform the wearer, Diana Vreeland firmly believed that the magazine should have the ability to transport the reader into an aesthetically perfect dream world.

Anna Wintour joined Condé Nast on the throne of *Vogue America* in 1988. Wintour's over 30-year reign has seen fashion's place in popular culture expand from a primarily female-focused niche to a global pop culture mainstay. In her early career, Anna Wintour embodied an era of dominance of the trade press, an era that would define the way fashion was represented for decades to come. *Vogue*'s success was partly built on selling glossy elitism to the masses.

Before the internet took readers away from the press, Condé Nast was known for hefty magazines edited by cultural arbiters who frequented the same circles as the people portrayed on their pages. They would feature glossy images, perfect bodies and dreamlike places with the aim of creating the extraordinary. This aim would inextricably link print media, fashion and luxury brands until the advent of social media.

Luxury lies in the realm of the extraordinary and this in itself creates desire. Economically, it's about price and value; culturally, it's about the magical aura that brands radiate; socially, it's about status and exclusivity; psychologically, it's about how a brand and its representation make people feel special. Luxury brands have known this for a long time. In their advertisements they generate desire based on three principles: enrichment, distancing and abstraction.

With respect to the mass market and premium brands, the differences are striking. Through storytelling, luxury brands lead us on a journey to the destination of desire, staking everything on the illusion of exclusivity. We rarely want what we can have immediately. That is why we seldom desire the ordinary world. Desire is created when something is out of reach.

As digital media advanced, Condé Nast and the other major traditional fashion publishers were slow to adapt. Due to

Diana Vreeland and Anna Wintur, legendary directors of *Vogue America*.

social media, internet access and a generational shift, consumers have become less interested in unattainable shiny dreams. The difference compared to the last century is that today, this hyper-consumption is being photographed with an iPhone and posted on Instagram.

Today, excessive spending is everywhere, in the media and on the web, and democratisation has somewhat normalised it, not least because of the vast array of outlet and resale sites that make big fashion brands accessible to many. Rather than exclusivity, today we talk about the principles of authenticity and community being upheld by the younger generations; rather than fixating on aspirational strategies through super premium images, big brands have turned to ideals linked to value and culture, to perfected lifestyles.

WHAT WOMEN WANT.
BRANDING AND
COMMUNICATION

For the love of the brand.
Identity, values and traditions

We live in the golden age of the brand. In the era of consumption, no product on the market is without one, but the history of brands dates back centuries.

"What's in a name? That which we call a rose, by any other name would smell as sweet." Thus reflected the legendary English playwright William Shakespeare in the late 1550s. "What's in a name?" In the luxury fashion brand scene, the "name" or "brand" is everything [1].

The history of brands dates back to ancient times, when it was customary to imprint the owner's name or a distinctive mark on livestock to differentiate between animals. This system was also used to distinguish the most select farms, helping customers make targeted purchasing decisions.

From the end of the 18th century onwards, the idea was further enhanced by the advent of the industrial revolution; during this era, the names of cities appeared as part of numerous brand symbols. The idea came not only from the need to indicate the product's origin, but also from the desire to emphasise its quality. Tea makers such as Twinings of England introduced branded products as early as 1706: English tea has always been considered the best.

Even men's tailors favoured insignias that looked British, while women's tailors sounded French by virtue of the fashion tradition that was already established in Paris. Branding as we know it today has evolved from a rudimentary concept of product differentiation to a refined business idea that is indispensable for any company wishing to create long-term value.

[1] Okonkwo, 2007.

Between the 18th and 19th centuries, new production processes triggered the advent of mass production. More products meant more consumer choice and, since companies had more competitors, the need to distinguish themselves became imperative. A trademark consists of legally registered words, phrases, symbols, designs, shapes and colours that identify a seller's company, product, goods or services, differentiating them from the competition. It could be Chanel's double "C" embossed on its handbags, Bottega Veneta's iconic weave design or Nike's Swoosh logo featured on the side of its shoes.

Registered trademarks rose to prominence in the 1870s, and the United States Congress approved its first trademark in 1881. But the world record goes to the Czech Republic, which in 1859 registered the Pilsner Bier trademark that is still in use today. According to historians, this was the first example of trademarks as intellectual property, which gave companies the opportunity to officially claim their products against fakes, copies and rivals.

The 20th century began with the birth of some iconic companies that would later become leading brands around the world. Coca-Cola (founded 1886), Colgate (1873), Ford Motor Company (1903), Chanel (1909) and LEGO (1932) were all pioneers, creators of one-of-a-kind brands. At the time of their creation, these brands were ahead of their time.

The Ford Motor Company was offering American-made gasoline-powered vehicles before anyone else. In the 1920s, Chanel was making practical women's dresses in jersey, at a time when silks, satins and other sophisticated materials were a fashion must for ladies of the upper classes (many of Chanel's clients were shocked by her choice of a fabric that was traditionally used for men's underwear).

In fashion, more than in other sectors, the brand is a fundamental attribute, the value of which depends on the ability to attribute a soul and a heart to otherwise trivial objects. Today this is an obvious concept, but it is actually a relatively recent idea. Until not so long ago, all attention was focused on the product, its formal qualities and the brand was "little more than a name" [2].

[2] Corbellini, Saviolo, 2007.

Throughout the 20th century, brands could find a special place to express themselves in newspapers, using words and images to differentiate themselves and create an identity. While in the beginning, advertisements were often strictly informative, i.e. they gave an exact description of the functionalities and features of the products, over time they became more subtle and were able to transform a simple purchase of a pair of shoes from something necessary for walking outside the home "into meaningful behaviour" [3].

Radio and television in the 1920s contributed to the development of increasingly sophisticated branding techniques. Through the use of jingles, slogans and targeted messages, in 1930 nearly 90% of radio stations in the United States were broadcasting commercials. Sponsorships and advertising took the concept of brand identity to a whole new level.

The brand becomes audible, memorable and recognisable. After radio comes television. On 1st July 1941, Bulova Watches air the first television commercial before a baseball game in New York. As television rapidly grew in popularity, companies began to exploit the new medium by sponsoring shows and creating ad hoc commercials. Through television, brands entered viewers' homes with images, words, sounds and music, bringing them closer to consumers than ever before.

The post-World War II period saw a radical transformation in both production and consumer culture. In the United States and Europe, the explosion of the middle class, suburbanisation and the widespread diffusion of television multiplied business opportunities. Billboards, underground and bus stop signs, "sponsored" buildings, sophisticated packaging and more and more advertising characterises the growth of all media. It was during this time that brand management develops as a discipline, with legions of brand managers engaged in creating specific identities for their products. A change characterised by a shift to more emotional advertising. Since competitors offered largely the same product, marketers had to differentiate themselves in other ways.

By studying target consumers, experts in the discipline developed a deeper understanding of the target audience,

[3] Fabris, Minestroni, 2004, p.20.

Left: L. Cappiello, Magazzini Mele
advertisement, Naples, 1904.
Right: M. Dudovich, La Rinascente
advertisement, Milan, 1925.

allowing them to draw on their desires, needs and aspirations. With the right images and messages, marketers aimed to create an emotional connection between products and consumers. The brand changes from informative to intimate.

From the dawn of the digital age in the late 1990s onwards, branding, marketing and advertising practices differ from historical techniques in many ways. TV advertising wins over print advertising, but social media advertising outperforms them all.

Advertisers have more power, namely they have the ability to target a demographic group in a Facebook ad, they also rely heavily on data, not only demographic data but also data based on a user's browsing patterns, social media activity and online shopping behaviour.

Through apps, links and an endless supply of personalised hashtags, brands today have no shortage of ways to increase brand awareness. Many of them have learned to leverage their personal experience in retail stores. Canadian-American sports brand Lululemon, for example, enhances its image by offering free yoga classes both in its stores and online.

In 2018, Gucci revived an old industrial space on Wooster Street in New York's Soho district, transforming it into a new centre dedicated to art and fashion. On the surface, it is simply a boutique, but in addition to selling the latest collections designed by Alessandro Michele, it aims to involve customers in the particular narrative of the Florentine brand, celebrating its artistic and artisanal character. The space is aimed at entertaining by hosting ad hoc presentations and events.

The ability to create emotions is increasingly important and, today more than ever, consumers are looking for products that allow them to "get in touch with their spiritual side" [4]. It is no longer a question of buying something to satisfy objective needs, but rather of sharing values, of responding to emotional needs.

The aim is to create brand knowledge, meaning the degree to which consumers are aware of a brand, what thoughts, feelings and images it evokes about experiences associated with a brand [5], which translates into greater brand loyalty.

[4] Cappellari, p. 59.
[5] Kotler, 2015.

Gucci concept store in Wooster
Street, Soho, New York.

Style star. The creative director and the cult of personality

The history of fashion is a story about people. In the last century, it was the couturiers and designers who laid the foundations of the fashion industry as we know it today. The liberation of women from the constraints of corsets, the invention of ready-to-wear clothing, logos, licences, window displays, brands, fashion shows, marketing and even the protection of intellectual property rights, are all vital elements of the modern fashion system, each the result of the courage and creative genius of individuals who have gone down in history as innovators and visionaries. Fashion is not just about fabric, it is also and above all about dreams.

Within a century, the idea of a designer went from being a simple tailor working in the backrooms of a workshop, sewing and basting, to a paradigm of creativity, fame and wealth. Rose Bertin is considered the first internationally renowned seamstress. Nicknamed the Minister of Fashion, she was the personal dressmaker of Marie Antoinette,

Queen of France from 1770 to 1793, a relationship destined for history. When Bertin opened a shop in Paris, her creations had considerable influence on the Parisian style of the time, until the French Revolution forced her into exile in London.

Rose Bertin was a *marchande de mode*, a creator, a visionary, rather than a simple seamstress or milliner. Her duties included, first and foremost, anticipating the desires of her wealthy clients, and supervising the making of garments and accessories with the addition of sumptuous quantities of embroidery, lace, ribbons and other trimmings. On her hats, the ornamentation was even more inventive, with feathers, fruit and flowers. But nothing was more imaginative than her *pouf* designs. The elaborate hairstyles in vogue among the Parisian nobility were the most extreme example of the excesses achieved by fashion during that period.

As a fashion consultant to the Queen of France, Bertin was instrumental in defining the extravagant fashions of the time. Her influence on Marie Antoinette's style earned the queen the title of first fashion victim in history. Indeed, France's first minister of fashion, an unofficial title at court, boasted international influence. At the height of her career, Rose Bertin had over 1,500 clients from some of the richest families in the world. In addition to Marie Antoinette, she dressed the queens of Spain, Sweden and Portugal, as well as numerous other members of the aristocracy.

After her, it was Charles Frederick Worth (1825-1895), an Englishman living in Paris, who would lead the way in the evolution of fashion. Worth is considered the first designer in the modern sense of the word, at a time when the fashion world was dominated by individual seamstresses – always women – who would create clothes according to the wishes of their wealthy customers. He was the owner of a business that employed staff, including many tailors, most of whom were anonymous. Never before in the fashion world had a man embarked on such a career. Worth was the first fashion designer to dictate style, steering the direction of tastes and trends. His popularity became overwhelming.

As Empress Eugenie's principal designer and a skilled businessman, Worth exploited his royal connections to gain

Examples of *poufs*, 1775-1780.

Élisabeth Vigée Le Brun, *Marie
Antoinette with a Rose*, 1783,
Château de Versailles.

recognition and increase his clientele, of which he was very
selective. Ladies who were not considered worthy of his designs were unceremoniously left at the door.

It is said that the couturier, accompanied by members of
his staff, regularly visited Eugénie at the palace to discuss
new models and designs. They didn't always agree, but the
designer's ideas prevailed more often than not. "Worth never wanted to change his ideas, it was almost impossible to
convince him to accept a modification or change in one of
his outfits."

As a rule, it was the sovereign who yielded (from Worth's
obituary, printed in the French newspaper *Le Gaulois*, 11th
March 1895. p. 1). It was a temperament that would earn
Worth the nickname, "the tyrant of fashion". In 1868, as a
direct result of the Empress's patronage, Maison Worth had

become the epicentre of good taste and elegance, even beyond the borders of Europe.

Having abandoned the modesty of executive tailoring, fashion would never be the same after Worth. The first novelty introduced by the designer was the idea of the fashion house itself. Clients were greeted at the door by young, well-mannered men in elegant suits, and having climbed the grand staircase covered with a thick red carpet and flanked by exotic plants, Worth's wealthy clients could sit in the large, well-lit salons on the upper floors.

The first room, sparsely furnished with a few chairs and display cases, contained only black and white silks. A second room, called the Rainbow Room, displayed silks of all colours and a third contained elaborate fabrics such as velvet and brocade. Then there was the analogue of today's showroom, where all the latest creations were displayed along a wall of mirrors. The last room, called the Salon des Lumières, was lit with artificial light, thereby offering customers the opportunity to try on their chosen outfit in a setting similar to that of an evening event.

Another innovation that made Worth particularly popular, and laid the foundations for haute couture as we know it today, was his decision to use new distribution techniques. As early as 1855, he agreed to sell some of his patterns to foreign buyers, along with the right to distribute them. Worth's most original creations could therefore easily be found throughout Europe and, by the mid-1860s, on the American market as well. "My business is not only to execute but especially to invent", he once said.

Worth was also among the first to sew labels on his clothes, showing himself to be a pioneer in understanding the benefits of marketing and branding: his clothes were designed to appeal to a wider customer base. Always highly recognisable, his designs aimed to make a visible statement about the client's style, elegance, fashionability and wealth.

"I thought it was best to make a good impression at the start, so I put on my prettiest gown," wrote American socialite Lillie Moulton [6] in her memoirs. "If one could see the waist band, one would read Worth in big letters."

[6] Hegermann-Lindencrone, 2015, pp. 26-29.

Three-piece ball gown, Maison Worth.

The most successful creations were then replicated at the end of the season and sold as ready-to-wear garments on the racks of major department stores in Paris, London and New York. In the mid-19th century, department stores as we know them today were at the beginning of their history, but they were rapidly becoming more popular.

Printemps and Samaritaine, still Parisian landmarks to-day, opened in the French capital in 1865. In London, Har-rods was already well established, in New York the Marble Palace owned by Alexander Turney Stewart opened near Broadway in 1848. With Worth, the era of traditional tailor-ing disappeared forever and the paradigm of the wealthy, successful designer entered the scene, paving the way for legendary figures whose names still represent fame and power today.

For much of the 20th century, the fashion industry continued to evolve thanks those who set the pace. In the United States, apart from the few pioneers of the first half of the century, including Adrian, Bonnie Cashin and Claire McCardell, the personalities behind the American fashion industry operated largely anonymously compared to their Parisian counterparts, where Coco Chanel, Alix Grès and Madeleine Vionnet had already become internationally renowned celebrities.

In the post-war period and the 1950s, however, more and more designers with entrepreneurial flair and creative genius started to come out of the back rooms, making a fortune thanks to their names being printed on the clothing labels. This evolution was facilitated in part by the curiosity of the press and also by manufacturers' ambitions to capitalise on the personalities of individual designers. One example, above all others, was Christian Dior. In ten short years, he would revitalise and revolutionise the fashion industry.

When he burst onto the Paris scene in 1947, his New Look created an international frenzy that had never been seen before. At the age of 41, with his idea of renewed femininity synthesised in the Corolle line, the designer helped to guide a world devastated by war into a new era of glamour and luxury. A few weeks after his debut collection, everyone knew Christian Dior, his look and his style. In 1950, the Christian Dior fashion house, founded only three years earlier with the support of entrepreneur Marcel Boussac, was earning more than half of the profits of the entire Parisian fashion industry.

Monsieur Dior's dresses appeared on the cover of *Life Magazine*, while the trade press turned him into a legend. Princesses and movie stars were falling over themselves for his latest designs. For a society beaten down by war, the opulence and femininity of the Corolle line represented a radical change of perspective, a fashion renaissance, and in a matter of hours, the contents of women's wardrobes around the world became obsolete. Carmel Snow, the legendary editor-in-chief at *Harper's Bazaar*, called the

debut collection a New Look. Reported by Reuters, these words renamed the line, thereby creating the legend.

Before Dior, the latest fashion trends would be introduced gradually, and new collections were little different from those of previous seasons. The seasonal and radical changes embraced by the Christian Dior fashion house, however, are unprecedented. Revered by the press, the stylist quickly becomes an international celebrity. The French fashion house was also the first to reap large profits from the use of licensing. Wholesale fashion companies could buy certain Dior patterns, in order to reproduce them on the mass market. In 1957, the Christian Dior fashion house licensed companies in eighty-seven countries to market the label on socks, bags, make-up and perfumes. Fashion as a large-scale multi-million dollar business was only just beginning.

In the long history of fashion, perhaps no one embodies the soul of their brand like Gabrielle Chanel. She was the one who carved a niche for the modern working woman and lived her own brand by wearing its practical clothes, small jackets and jersey fabric. Her simple garments speak of elegance and ease at the same time, maintaining the impeccable effect of bespoke tailoring, without however undermining the joy of femininity thanks to the frivolous delight of costume jewellery. The brand's values – elegance, practicality, quality, attention to detail and less-is-more approach – along with Madame Chanel's own personality, have led the brand to global success.

On the wave of economic development in the 1970s and 1980s, designers become real celebrities, ambitious and charismatic personalities at the head of commercial empires, the incarnation of the labels that bear their names. Ralph Lauren, Calvin Klein, Giorgio Armani, Gianni Versace are just some of the biggest names in fashion, and are still symbols of status and wealth today. Stefano Dolce, Domenico Gabbana and Marc Jacobs are among the latest examples of personalities that have become symbols of their brands. But in the last decade, under the auspices of the big luxury conglomerates LVMH, Kering and Richemont, the "cult of personality" of the fashion designer has undergone a radical change.

It is no longer a question of creating large fashion houses under the name and leadership of a single charismatic personality (the last being Marc Jacobs himself, with his label founded in 1984 and taken over by LVMH in 1997). Today, hiring famous designers with million-dollar contracts helps brands renew a worn-out image, turning fans of those designers into new buyers for the fashion house.

As of the beginning of 2018, the fashion industry has seen two major new celebrity designer "hires". The first being Yves Saint Laurent star Hedi Slimane who moved on to Celine, immediately achieving recognition by turning the brand into "his Celine". This meant changing the logo, in order to remove all trace of the previous designer Phoebe Philo's legacy from the brand. The style was also initially altered dramatically, but was soon brought back into line following protests from those who were fond of the practicality and sophisticated style that "old Celine" embodied. In March 2018, British fashion brand Burberry recruited Riccardo Tisci from Givenchy, granting the Italian designer the power to run the entire fashion house, as well as inventing a new logo, a new monogram and a programme linked to distinguished capsule editions.

Chanel outfits, 1920s.

In 2020, after seasons of declining sales, Prada announced the "purchase" of Raf Simons, another golden boy on the contemporary fashion scene, with the mission of bringing new creative life (and new customers) to the historic brand led by Miuccia. From Slimane to Tisci and Simons, the preferences and values of these designers are firmly intertwined with the brands' actions and identities. Today, more than ever, a brand has to stand for something, it is no longer just about heritage, craftsmanship and creativity, it is also and above all about values.

Some of the historic products guaranteed by Royal Warrants.

The power of stardom.
Hollywood, Royals and power stylists

You only have to walk into a shopping centre, scroll through Instagram or flip through any fashion magazine to realise this. Celebrities are everywhere. The endorsement of actors, models and music stars has always been a successful marketing strategy in many industries. More than any other industry, the world of fashion revolves around stars and while in the last century celebrities were much more likely to appear on cereal boxes than on magazine covers, today things have changed a lot.

Advertising linked to famous names and faces has actually been prevalent since the Middle Ages. A prime example being Royal Warrants, which were a mark of recognition of royal approval conferred to a manufacturer by British kings and queens, before the practice spread throughout Europe. Royal Warrants are still granted by Queen Elizabeth II and the Prince of Wales to companies or traders who provide out-

By Appointment to
HM The Queen

By Appointment to
HRH The Duke of Edinburgh

By Appointment to
HRH The Prince of Wales

Royal Warrant Crests.

standing goods and services to royal households. The warrant allows the supplier to advertise that they have been selected by the royal family for the quality of the products offered.

It is in fact a mark that allows companies to display the royal coat of arms outside shops, factories and sometimes on the product itself – because if it is approved by a royal it will certainly be the best available on the market. From porcelain to food, clothing and stationery, the use of the crown emblem has for centuries given brands and products a touch of prestige.

Between 1875 and 1900, trade cards were invented as a precursor to modern advertising. These were slips of paper inserted into the packaging of the products being sold, and a photograph of a celebrity would often accompany the advertised products. Actresses such as Lily Langtry and Sarah Bernhardt, and baseball players such as Cy Young, Babe Ruth and Ty Cobb were the first to put their fame to commercial use. Writer Mark Twain, famous author of *The Adventures of Tom Sawyer* and *Adventures of Huckleberry Finn*, was so famous that he appeared simultaneously in several campaigns promoting cigarettes, spirits, clothing and, not surprisingly, fountain pens. Celebrity support in the fashion industry is not a new phenomenon.

Charles F. Worth, the man who invented haute couture in Paris in the 19th century, understood the importance of linking a famous face to the brand long before it became an important communication and marketing tool. To promote his fashion house, Worth chose a woman of high society

Spice Girls for Pepsi advertising campaign, 1997.

and influential court fashionista, Princess Von Metternich, wife of the then Austrian ambassador to France and a close friend of Napoleon's wife, Empress Eugenie. This celebrity's patronage and connection with Maison Worth contributed greatly to the success and status of the French fashion house as the most influential in the world at the time.

The celebrity endorser is defined as "a person who enjoys public recognition and uses his or her fame on behalf of a consumer good by appearing with it in an advertisement" [7]. Their image, presumed characteristics and the idea that the public has cultivated about them, is transferred in the advertising to the sponsored product. Several studies have shown that celebrities can have a direct positive impact on the success of an advertising campaign and an indirect effect on brand perception and purchase intentions [8].

In 1984, for example, Pepsi attributed the 8% increase in sales to Michael Jackson's endorsement for a payment of US$20 million. In 1997, thanks to the Spice Girls, the global market share increased by 2% [9].

Celebrities are people who exert significant influence in different aspects of society in the fields of art, music, film and television, sports, culture, politics and even religion. They range from film and television stars to musicians, sports personalities, royalty, politicians and even socialites with undefined careers.

In the world of fashion, the list of celebrities includes designers and their muses, models, photographers and any

[7] McCracken, G., "Who Is the Celebrity Endorser? Cultural Foundations of the Endorsement Process", *Journal of Consumer Research*, vol. 16, n. 3, 1989, pp. 310-321.

[8] Pelsmacker et al., "Consumer Values and Fair-trade Beliefs, Attitudes and Buying Behaviour", *International Review on Public and Nonprofit Marketing*, n. 2, 2005, pp. 50-69.

[9] Erdogan, B. Z., Baker, M. J., "Towards a Practitioner-based Model of Selecting Celebrity endorsers", *International Journal of Advertising*, n. 19 (1), 2000, pp. 25-42.

Michael Jordan for Nike.

prominent person involved in the creative arts, such as make-up artists and consultants. The most popular celebrities used in promoting fashion brands are those of the film and music industries, because of how important the role of image and personal style is in these entertainment sectors.

The 1980s saw the start of the era of millionaire sponsorship with Michael Jordan. His US$2.5 million deal with Nike, signed in 1984, included the exclusive supply of bespoke Air Jordans, the first shoe to associate a brand with the athletic attributes of a specific NBA sportsman. At a rate of US$65 per pair, Nike grossed US$70 million in the first year after launch. Almost forty years later, Jordan regularly collects US$100 million annually in royalties from the legendary sneakers that bear his name.

Brooke Shields for the Calvin Klein Jeans advertising campaign, 1995.

In 1995, Calvin Klein chose a very young Brooke Shields, then fifteen years old, to star in its controversial campaign. The iconic slogan "Do you know what comes between me and my Calvins?" would contribute to a substantial increase in sales and lasting success for the American brand. Choosing to use a testimonial from a famous person makes the advertising more visible and consolidates the popularity of the brand. Between 2005 and 2006 Versace hired pop star Madonna, and Hollywood actresses Demi Moore and Halle Berry.

With the choice of a testimonial, the celebrity's style and behaviour are consistent with the brand image and the target audience, and the possibility of consumers identifying with it further strengthens the message. In 2004, the advertising campaign for Chanel N.° 5 centred on an almost three-minute short film directed by *Moulin Rouge* director Baz Luhrmann starring Nicole Kidman. This was the turning point for a new kind of marketing approach for luxury products. The idea of linking the object, and consequently the brand, to an emotional story would be a global trend from then on.

This cinematic approach created a very solid bond with consumers, but at a very high price, commensurate with the turnover of the French fashion house. The investment included Kidman's £18 million contract, five couture gowns made for the film, her diamond necklace, production costs and so on, as part of Chanel's desire to position N.° 5 as "the perfume par excellence on the market".

Another example of celebrity endorsement is the use of sponsored products and brands in films and TV programmes: in 1980, *American Gigolo* was a veritable showcase for Giorgio Armani's clothes and contributed to the global success of the Italian brand. The same happened with Manolo Blahnik and Jimmy Choo in the hit series *Sex and the City* with Carrie Bradshaw alias Sarah Jessica Parker. One rule above all others is that the chosen celebrity must be credible, boasting a high level of competence and talent in their field. These merits add value to the brand and indicate an intention to be associated with the best.

Any mismatch between brands and celebrities or any misconduct in the latter's private life can instantly destroy a brand's reputation, just as an actor's career can be short-

Manolo Blahnik for *Sex and the City*.

lived if undermined by private misdeeds. Nonetheless, the industry is thriving, social networks, Instagram in particular, have only accelerated the trend with a new wave of influencers replacing expensive traditional celebrities in many cases. Promotional tweets, paid posts on Instagram and Facebook and other types of sponsorship are added to the recipe, along with new media channels and apps.

The British phenomenon of royal influencers, boasting a history spanning over a century, deserves a separate mention. Starting with Queen Alexandra, fashion icon and pioneer of aristocratic style, up to the royal wedding of the century between Meghan Markle and Prince Harry in 2018. The worldwide fascination with royalty

Royal Wedding between Prince Harry and Meghan Markle, 2018.

is stronger than ever and the current appetite for fairy tales with happy endings at a time of historical uncertainty seems to justify this trend.

In 2017, a report by *Lyst*, the global fashion research platform funded by luxury giant LVMH, analysed the influence British royal women have had on fashion over the past one hundred years. The site recorded real-time peaks in online searches and sales whenever a so-called "blue-blooded" influencer was wearing a certain brand. The result? Famous families such as the Kardashians and the Hadids count for little in comparison with the extraordinary public interest generated whenever a member of the Windsor family makes a public appearance. Each new frock worn by the latest crowned sweetheart unleashes an unprecendented frenzy; the outfit is guaranteed to be sold out in no time and profits soar.

Identity for sale.
Communication in the world of the image

Our sense of ourselves is constantly evolving, but values and aspirations are so deeply connected to individual identity that they manifest themselves independently of context. Today's consumer no longer dreams of owning something, but of being someone.

This is why the strategies of fashion brands – cosmetic products in particular – appeal to a person's psychological, social and economic aspirations, positioning a product or service through use of images, to assert an ideal. Fashion and beauty brands have always emphasised the aesthetics of perfection. The incarnation of perfection, however, can change over time – from Marilyn Monroe's blonde hair, to Naomi Campbell's toned figure, to Kim Kardashian's curves – and is based on the idea that women must conform to a certain idealised standard in order to be considered attractive.

Beauty is cultural. What one community admires can leave another indifferent. What one individual finds irresistible

Inclusive advertising by Oliviero Toscani for Benetton.

UNITED COLORS OF BENETTON.

may be of no interest to others. Beauty is personal, but it is also universal. There are internationally recognised beauties who have come to embody the standard. For generations, beauty has required a slim build, but with generous breasts and a narrow waist. The jaw had to be defined, the cheekbones high and sharp. The nose had to be angular. Features had to be symmetrical; lips full; eyes, ideally blue or green, had to be large and bright. Hair had to be long, thick and flowing, and preferably golden. Above all else, the model had to be young.

Since the appearance of women's magazines, beauty has been codified and commercialised; the aforementioned characteristics became a yardstick, something to aspire to. This cliché is so ingrained in popular culture that so-called beauty icons – universally admired women such as the actress Marilyn Monroe, Princess Grace of Monaco or the top model Claudia Schiffer – are still examples of notable charm and attractiveness. With the perfect version being white, blond and slender, straying too far from the standards meant being less attractive and desirable. For some women, whether they were no longer very young, had dark skin or soft curves, beauty seemed an unattainable goal.

On an emotional level, being perceived as attractive means being welcomed into the conversation, being part of the advertising and marketing audience. Several theories on advertising ethics have been based on the general distinction between informative and persuasive advertisements. The main differences in these techniques relate to the ways in which each one provides information. Informative advertising also uses persuasive techniques, but is based more on facts, whereas persuasive advertising tries to arouse emotions in order to make the sale.

Fashion, for obvious reasons, has always resorted to persuasive advertising. Fashion ads aim to persuade by presenting idealised images, such as a sexy teenager (Calvin Klein) or a young, beautiful, rich and somewhat rebellious girl (Chanel). The product becomes a symbol of the ideal and target consumers are invited to use the product in order to project that image onto themselves and others.

Numerous studies have highlighted the negative effects that images used by the fashion and beauty industry have caused for generations, particularly on women, by promoting unrealistic standards, lowering self-esteem and self-perception. These effects create a strong need in the consumer to continuously purchase products, in order to fit the aesthetic ideals of modern society.

Fashion still predominantly presents impeccable, tendentially Eurocentric images of very slim, very young models. However, fashion consumers fall into all categories of age, shape, size and skin tone. Most of them are still poorly represented in fashion images and, for many, such marginalisation leads to feelings of insecurity.

For decades, the industry has been insensitive and prejudiced against underrepresented groups: the industry's problematic lack of diversity is not only racial, but may also reflect socio-economic inequalities.

Social media has partly changed the rules of the game: in a world where everyone has the opportunity to advertise themselves, differences and imperfections have undermined the advertising ideal of female perfection, which is now less obvious and more diverse than ever.

In the 21st century, a typical consumer can no longer relate to the refined fantasy world of commercials made of hair spray and porcelain skin. In the global marketplace, social media has propagated fashion – and its critics – faster and more widely than ever before. For future-oriented brands in a hyper-connected world, impeccable ethical, cultural and environmental conduct has become a must. Risks associated with declining reputation due to insensitive mistakes can lead to boycotts and cost millions in lost revenue.

In the recent long series of fashion faux pas, the case of Dolce & Gabbana remains emblematic. Three videos, released in November 2018, showed a Chinese model struggling with chopsticks trying to eat Italian food including cannoli, pizza and spaghetti. Chinese culture attaches particular importance to the ritual of the meal, which is regulated by a precise *etiquette* that prohibits, for example, stabbing the food. In these advertising spots, every cultural meaning was distorted and openly mocked, which is why it was considered very offensive and disrespectful. This led to a strong backlash on the Chinese market, with many retailers deciding to withdraw the Italian brand's products from sale.

The Dolce & Gabbana incident is a cautionary tale. While it remains difficult to calculate the amount of money lost as a result of such a scandal, the serious reputational damage remains a fact. In a context where consumers, especially in the high-end market, are increasingly attentive to a brand's intangible qualities (what it stands for, its values and moral conduct) in addition to the product itself, reputation becomes a very valuable asset.

In 2019, Gucci, Prada and Moncler had to withdraw products from the market that evoked stereotypes related to the representation of black faces; while many, including Gucci, Chanel and Burberry, rushed to hire staff responsible for diversity and inclusion within their respective companies in order to avoid possible scandals.

After years of complacency, the fashion industry is facing a perfect storm of political awareness, activism and information that is putting pressure on brands to step up their efforts to operate flawlessly. The rise of social media and a

Dolce & Gabbana, Abaya line
dedicated to Muslim women, 2016.

Mohammed Hassan on Unsplash

changing cultural and political landscape have catapulted such conversations into the headlines: as a result, brands that are active in the globalised marketplace have equipped themselves so as not to betray the expectations of consumers who are increasingly diverse and informed.

It's not just about communication; the collections have also been expanded and adapted to capitalise on a broader and more diverse customer base. Following the accusation of almost exclusively serving an idealised Western, thin and slender consumer, while ignoring the physical characteristics and needs of the majority of the population, fashion houses have in recent years responded with targeted collections.

Established and emerging markets in Asia, Latin America and Africa, where the population has different physical characteristics to those of the Western ideal, have provided additional incentives. Plus size or curvy lines have become ubiquitous and there is also a growing awareness of the needs of consumers with mobility and health issues: in 2018, brands such as Nike, Tommy Hilfiger and Target began designing adaptive collections.

Numerous modest lines have been created for those who, either for religious beliefs or personal taste, prefer to avoid showing cleavage or baring their knees. It is not just a question of products, but also of turnover: consumers in Muslim countries, plus-size wearers and the adaptive sector con-

Tommy Hilfiger adaptive line advertisement.

stitute a large and potentially very profitable customer base that was ignored just a few years ago. For a sector founded on the sale of exclusivity, integrating the concept of inclusiveness has proved particularly challenging.

Behind the façade of its big glossy advertising campaigns, fashion is still struggling to adapt the way it operates to the challenges imposed by the global market. Major brands have been willing to bow to consumer demand in favour of more diverse faces, shapes and colours, but have been slow to embrace change at its roots: executives of the world's largest fashion companies remain mostly white and male. From 2016 onwards, the change was visible, albeit gradual.

In 2017, Edward Enninful became the first black editor-in-chief at *Vogue UK*. In 2018, with his shot of Beyoncé for the September issue, Tyler Mitchell became the first black photographer to shoot a cover of *Vogue America* in the magazine's history. That same year in Paris, Virgil Abloh became the first African-American man elected to the role of artistic director for a brand owned by luxury giant LVMH.

Diversity, inclusion and sustainability are trends that are here to stay. The pressure that fashion companies face to

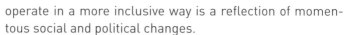

Edward Enninful on the cover of
Time, September 2020.

operate in a more inclusive way is a reflection of momentous social and political changes.

For years, fashion was able to propagate an exclusive – and for many unattainable – standard of beauty, but in the age of the internet, the market has demanded something else: while the web has created new opportunities on the one hand, it has also been a breeding ground for tricky pitfalls on the other.

In addition to the emergence of new sales platforms that are capable of reaching underserved emerging markets, the internet has revolutionised the way that fashions are communicated and disseminated, giving a voice to communities that were historically ignored by mainstream fashion.

The rise of the influencer phenomenon – figures who speak to a more diverse audience than the traditional fashion media can – has prompted brands to pay more attention and respond more quickly to requests for greater representation. The internet has also provided a strong platform for critical and activist voices that have been powerful in the efforts to push the industry along the path to inclusivity.

Activist campaigns such as "Who Made My Clothes", promoted by the Fashion Revolution organisation, have mobilised hundreds of thousands of consumers who are concerned about the working conditions and respecting the rights of workers involved in the complex global supply chain of fast fashion. Social media has changed the way brands and consumers interact with each other. Thanks to the power and popularity of Facebook and Instagram, customers share unfiltered feedback that is accessible to millions of users. In the age of social media, the customer has become an activist.

Beyoncé photographed by Tyler
Mitchell for *Vogue America*,
September 2018.

IT'S A MALL WORLD: RETAIL AND SHOPPING TEMPLES

A brief history of shopping

Coined in the unbridled 1980s, the term retail therapy perfectly illustrates the evolution of fashion shopping over the last hundred years: from a purely utilitarian act to a widespread mood-improving pastime. At some point in the history of fashion and society, shelling out for something new became synonymous with self-improvement, and was more powerful than any exercise, sunshine, or antidepressant. Or at least that's what advertising has led us to believe.

Speculation aside, historians and sociologists agree that from Victorian London to Soviet-era Moscow to the mega-malls of Dubai, department stores have changed the fashion industry, remodeled cities and helped shape global culture.

The title, The World's First Department Store belongs to Harding, Howell & Co's Grand Fashionable Magazine at 89 Pall Mall in St James's, London. Opened in 1796, this beautiful Georgian shop was divided into four departments crammed with furs and fans, haberdashery, jewellery, watches and hats. Harding, Howell & Co was all about the needs and desires of the fashionable women of the time.

In its halls, vibrant with golden light, ladies were free to browse and shop in a safe and honorable environment, away from home and the company of a man – at the time, a male chaperone was considered obligatory when appearing in public. The clientele was made up of middle-class women, whose fortunes – and that of the department store itself – were fuelled by the raging river that was the Industrial Revolution which, marked by free trade, mind-blowing inventions and steam, was by that point transforming the economy and society at a dizzying pace.

La Marchande de modes, engraving by Robert Bénard, 1769.

In the 18th century, fashion was no longer dictated by courts encumbered by centuries-old privileges, but by city streets dotted with shops to browse in, crowded with busy passers-by. In the Age of Enlightenment, fashion became part of consumption, no longer just the affair of the rich, but widespread among individuals of different social and economic backgrounds.

In history books, the 18th century is remembered for two crucial revolutions that transformed European history: the Industrial Revolution, which transformed the entire economy of the continent, and the French Revolution, which turned politics upside down. In recent years, scholars have started to investigate a third revolution, namely that of consumption. From 1700 onwards, consumerism would become a major social phenomenon in which the purchase of products, including clothing, became an integral part of the daily lives of thousands of people.

It would become a new pastime that was capable of defining an individual's identity. It was no longer a question of only buying basic necessities, but superfluous objects too, chosen for personal, intellectual and aesthetic pleasure. With the abandonment of DIY and sewing machines for making clothes at home, modern consumerism takes shape in the

Age of Enlightenment, thanks to some fundamental inventions: shops, advertising and marketing.

One of the engines of mass consumption was fashion [1], which, with its systematic "whims", tirelessly whetted the appetite for novelty. Far from remaining the prerogative of a few, it becomes accessible to different strata of society. The idea of going shopping became established in the 18th century, with the expansion of fixed spaces that were suitable for displaying clothes and accessories.

Fashion doesn't just need to be admired and desired in shops, but in newspapers and magazines where it can be talked about, too. From chaotic street vendors to illuminated shop windows. Indeed, artisanal shops already existed in the Middle Ages – think of cities such as Florence and Venice – but in the 18th century, shops became defined spaces, separated from the street and equipped with display windows.

In the centuries that followed, shop display windows became the symbol of modern consumerism, combining objects, desire and voyeurism. The first shops were not specialised, but were rather spaces dedicated to the sale of various kinds of merchandise, but as demand and competition increased, product specialisation took over.

Harry Gordon Selfridge (1858-1947) and his department store on Oxford Street, London.

Opposite: Harrods department store, founded in 1834 in London, still today a luxury shopping destination.

[1] McKendrick, Brewer, Plumb, 1982.

Le Bon Marché, Paris, 1853.

The streets of central Paris in the 19th century, for example, were home to numerous *marchandes de mode*: shops for hats and small accessories, the ancestors of modern department stores. The development of department stores is linked to the growth of large population centres, as well as transport and electricity for power and lighting, during the 19th century. It is no coincidence that from the mid-19th century onwards (more than 150 years), department stores adopted the appearance we know today.

In London, many of the first department stores, such as John Lewis and Whiteleys, were founded by cloth merchants, the first to capture the tastes and imagination of the emerging new generation of middle-class women. The story of Harry Gordon Selfridge, a Wisconsin-born retailer who left school at the age of 14 to deliver newspapers, has become a legend.

First a salesman and later a partner at Marshall Field in Chicago (a company founded in 1852, one of the earliest and most ambitious American department stores), Mr. Sel-

Malgorzata Bujalska on Unsplash

Interior of one of the departments in Harrods.

fridge was surprised to find, while on holiday in London in 1906, that the famous British city lacked large glamorous spaces for fashion sales, despite the fact that Harrods had just completed its Knightsbridge building. So he decided to leave the States and open the legendary department store at the western end of Oxford Street in the city.

The initial project was by American architect Daniel Burnham. The idea was to design a luxurious classical palace, the kind usually intended for the Fine Arts; a prestigious building, illuminated by a wall of mirrored windows. Opened in 1909, Selfridges offered its lucky customers a hundred or so retail spaces along with restaurants, tea rooms, a roof garden, reading lounges, reception areas for foreign visitors, a first aid station and, above all, a small army of experienced sales assistants who served as guides for those who wanted to discover the most luxurious goods.

Selfridge went to great lengths to make the department store a destination rather than just a large, well-stocked

The Moscow GUM.

shop. His department store became a meeting place and entertainment venue for the rising middle class.

In Paris, Le Bon Marché is considered by many historians to be the very first shopping centre. It was founded in 1852, followed by Printemps (1865) and La Samaritaine (1869) and offered glamorous fashion items in sophisticated Art Nouveau and Art Deco settings. In his 1883 novel *The Ladies' Paradise*, Émile Zola defined department stores as "cathedrals of commerce"; their sumptuous architecture served as an advertisement for the products sold inside.

Over the course of just over two centuries, the department store formula proved so attractive that it was replicated in all major Western cities – even in Lenin's socialist Russia. The GUM (State Department Store) in Moscow's Red Square dates back to 1921. For Lenin, it was a showcase of "socialist consumerism". Unsurprisingly, the impressive-looking store only sold goods from Soviet factories.

In Italy, La Rinascente boasts a history of more than 150 years. Founded by the Bocconi brothers in 1865, it took its current name in 1917, thanks to Gabriele D'Annunzio's intuitiveness. La Rinascente in Milan's Piazza Duomo was the scene of some major fashion revolutions, for example, it was the first store in Italy to sell the miniskirt.

During the 19th and 20th centuries, the largest department store chains in the world were inaugurated in the United States: Macy's in 1858, Bloomingdale's in 1861, Saks Fifth Avenue in 1867, Bergdorf Goodman in 1899, Nordstrom in 1901, Neiman Marcus in 1907 and Barneys in 1923. Their primary purpose was still to sell, but in the history of fashion the big American department stores played a fundamental role in deciding what was in and what was out: the sceptre of power was in the hands of the buyers – it was up to them and the trade press to decide on the success or failure of a brand. Ralph Lauren, for example, owes the beginnings of his fortune to Bloomingdale's, the American department store that was the first to sell his initial creations: colourful "Polo" brand ties.

Bloomingdale's, Lexington Avenue, New York City.

If the conditions for the rise of the department store lay in the industrialisation and urbanisation of the late 18th and early 19th centuries, the end of the golden age of the American department store has been brought about by the advent of the internet, online shopping and a substantial change in the habits and tastes of shoppers around the world. The size of shopping malls continued to increase throughout the 20th and into the 21st century.

Today, the largest in the world reside in the Middle East and the trend has shifted from the department store to the mall which, unlike its predecessor, is much larger and consists of several buildings housing independent shops rather than just departments. More and more, they are as large as small towns and host everything you need for entertainment purposes – whether you need to buy anything or not, as this is not the point of the experience. The Dubai Mall in the United Arab Emirates, with its 12 million square metres, is the grandest of them all.

Interior of the Dubai Mall.

Mostafa Meraji on Unsplash

Merchandising and consumption

Merchandising is as old as commerce itself, but the promotion of goods through their presentation at the point of sale has become a fine art. Once simple window dressers – the great Giorgio Armani actually began his stellar career in this role for Rinascente – today, merchandisers are creative professionals who do more than just design and install shop windows and retail environments. The work includes strategic analysis, marketing, management and distribution of products in order to maximise profits. Their choices involve virtually every aspect of the fashion industry, from design to sales, with the aim of increasing profits through trend analysis, purchasing, inventory management and marketing.

In recent years, the internet has revolutionised the way brands and retailers think about sales: it is no longer a question of launching new trends, but of following consumer tastes by designing clothes that are expected to be commercially successful. In short, it is about understanding what customers want to wear and for that to happen, having a crystal ball is not enough.

Traditionally, merchandisers worked separately from the design team, and were often brought in at the end of the process to determine the quantities to be produced and how to price them. In the case of catwalk collections, merchandising teams had the task of commercialising the garments presented during fashion weeks, which were often excessive and idealised.

But the internet has overturned the old rules. Trends move faster on the web and are more likely to be successful with a narrow demographic than with consumers as a whole. Shoppers are also less loyal to the brand and more price-conscious. At the heart of it is always an intelligent presentation of products, with the intention of touching the senses of potential customers, playing the right chords, arousing emotions in order to subtly persuade them to make an impulse buy.

Today's merchandisers provide the design team with information on trends and customer preferences, which can play a crucial role in creative decisions.

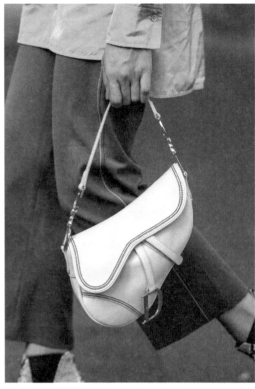

Left: Baguette by Fendi.
Right: Saddle bag by Dior.

Maria Grazia Chiuri, creative director of Dior since 2016, has often been portrayed in the press as a skilled merchandiser as well as a skilled designer. At the beginning of her career, she had the idea for the first "it-bag" in history: the Fendi Baguette. She was also responsible for the great commercial success of the historic French fashion house, Dior: its feminist slogans, and a well-thought-out revival of the legendary Saddle bag, created by Galliano in 1999, are just a few examples. The relaunch of the saddle-shaped bag in 2018 was accompanied by a coordinated blitz on Instagram, involving over 100 influencers. Despite astronomical prices, Chiuri works her magic on iconic yet easy-to-wear pieces.

Fashion merchandising is the study of trends to determine sales strategies for brands and retail stores. It is a field that requires both intuition and aesthetic sensibility as well as a shrewd understanding of business management. When we think of the fashion industry, design takes pride of place. Yet there is more to it than that: in the age of the global market, merchandising is almost as vital as the design itself.

Starchitects and brand image

Le Bon Marché Rive Gauche, considered by many historians to be the world's first modern department store, was opened in Paris in 1852 on the initiative of former provincial clerk Aristide Boucicaut and his wife Marguerite. In just a few years, thanks to a strong pricing policy and rapid stock turnover, profits soared from a few hundred francs to several million. Having achieved success, Monsieur Boucicaut decided on a radical restyling.

The idea was to create "a new kind of shop that would create great excitement". Architect Louis-Charles Boileau and illustrious engineer Gustave Eiffel, a master in the art of iron and crystal architecture, were hired for the project. With a desire to impress, the result was a huge building illuminated by large windows, a veritable cathedral of commerce. The idea of hiring a famous designer had proved successful. The slender iron column structure and skylight roof over the inner courtyards, which were innovative for the time and never before used in a commercial context, guaranteed a breathtaking effect.

Le Bon Maché Rive Gauche, today.

The space was very well laid out and the display changed frequently in order to encourage customers to come in time and again to check out all the new stock. Visiting department stores became such a popular activity for Parisians that it would later inspire the novel *The Ladies' Paradise* by Émile Zola. From 1870 onwards, the idea of shopping as entertainment provided the foundation of what would become modern retail.

One hundred and fifty years later, large department stores are no longer the number one favourite urban shopping destination. Changes ushered in by younger generations' shopping preferences, the internet and, last but not least, increasingly high running costs, have reduced the number (and tarnished the reputation) of department stores, especially in the United States.

But their lessons on how to entertain and win over customers remain as a reminder of their rich legacy. Today, the new retail frontier is undergoing an evolutionary phase whereby the store is no longer exclusively a place dedicated to shopping, but – once again – aims to offer a shopping experi-

Luxury shop, Dubai Mall.

Iwona Castiello D'antonio on Unsplash

Freestocks on Unsplash

ence that focuses on entertainment. Between commerce, art and hospitality, shops have become venues for exclusive events, receptions, presentations, private exhibitions and, of course, memorable shopping experiences.

In the luxury sector in particular, the purchase of clothing is much more than a simple transaction: in sophisticated boutiques, customers are greeted by an all-encompassing aesthetic experience in which clothing, design and architecture complement each other.

Despite the advance of online commerce, and the fact that many had already given up on retail stores, in-person shopping has become even more central to luxury brands' branding strategies. From architecture to staging, from lighting to materials, from background music to the shopping experience, boutiques are now unrivalled places where brands can best express their values as a tangible symbol of their prestige.

While many have placed their bets on increasingly digital-ised points of sale – the potential of which is still at an exper-imental stage – others have staked everything on strength-ening the traditional link between fashion, art, architecture and design, teaming up with world-famous starchitects, artists and interior designers to create megastores with a high visual impact. This relationship takes shape in what is known as a flagship store (a chain or brand's most im-portant store, which is located in a large city and has the highest sales volume).

For a retailer, opening a single-brand flagship store marks the first point in the development of a portfolio of shops within the most relevant foreign markets. Hence the funda-mental importance accorded to the layout and furnishings of these spaces: they are there first and foremost to amaze and excite, and then to sell.

At the end of the 20th century, the relationship between designers/managers and world-famous architects became one of the most fascinating aspects of major international brands' image strategies. The years between 1999 and 2007 saw the most ambitious, complex and expensive "signa-ture" structures ever to be built for fashion houses: highly customised spaces and entire buildings that mirrored the culture and prestige of the most famous brands.

Spectacular opening ceremonies became the norm in a sort of competition for the grandest project. Futuristic structures, breathtaking buildings and innovative layouts all hinted at substantial changes in the conception of the fashion business.

What was remarkable was not so much the renewed collab-oration between architects (who have now become veritable cultural stars) and designers/brands of immense renown, as the metamorphosis of the boutique from a sophisticated retail space into a place that was symbolic of and embodied brands' values and aesthetics.

In 2001, the first Prada Epicentre opened in New York's Soho district. Partly the ancestor of the Foundation of the same name, it was neither a gallery nor a cultural institu-tion, but a shop.

Interior of the Prada Epicenter,
Soho, New York.

Built in a space formerly belonging to the Guggenheim Museum, designed by the OMA studio, and managed by provocative Dutch architect Rem Koolhaas, the Prada Epicenter in New York is more like a space where you would admire works of art than clothes.

The vast building of over seven thousand square metres covers an entire block, but its interior is almost completely devoid of clothing. Those who walk through its doors are greeted by what Koolhaas calls the "wave", a wooden ramp that slopes down from street level to the lower level, and features motorised suspended cages for displays and a folding stage for special events.

Both the architecture and the layout of the building can be considered a piece of contemporary art in itself. New York's first Epicenter remains, to this day, one of the most successful Prada stores in the world. The idea came from a suspicion that customers were bored with the typical luxury shopping experience.

The New York Epicenter, for its part, was designed to make the experience of shopping for clothes and accessories anything but mundane. It seems somewhat paradoxical, but the fact that the clothes are secondary to the space remains one of its strengths: it is a very sophisticated lifestyle that is on sale here, not just products. By analysing global shopping trends and conceptualising new retail tools, the Milan fashion house has created an innovative shopping concept based on extraordinary architectural designs that are highly recognisable in the urban context. Conceived in 2000 and completed in 2003, almost at the same time as the opening of the Epicenter in New York, Prada opened its second project in Tokyo in collaboration with Swiss architects Herzog & de Meuron.

The reverence felt by the Japanese people for clothing designed by Miuccia Prada is reflected in the grandeur of the six-story free-standing building in the Aoyama district, which is one of the most distinctive architectural works of the Japanese metropolis. Inside, the building houses retail floors, lounges and event spaces that are designed, according to Ms Prada, "to experiment with new ideas and products and to stimulate interaction between the store and its customers". Last in chronological order, Prada's third Epicenter opens in Los Angeles in Rodeo Drive in 2004, designed by architect Rem Koolhaas to have a specific relationship with the New York store "through its horizontality and the need to connect two levels". Meanwhile in New York, a "wave" glides down to the basement; in Los Angeles, a wooden plane rises to create a symmetrical "hill" supporting a suspended aluminium box on the second floor.

Several years have passed since Prada's Epicentres in Los Angeles, Tokyo and New York were designed, and time has not affected their strategic importance: since then, architecture has become a significant communication tool for fashion brands; a confirmation of the new way to negotiate the changing mentality of evolved consumers who are looking for experiences as well as exclusive products.

Distribution plays a key role in the management of high-end and lifestyle products. Luxury fashion retailers tend to limit their direct representation of big brands to a "flagship"

Prada Epicenter, Tokyo.

store in the larger shopping cities. London's Bond Street, New York's Fifth Avenue, Milan's Via Montenapoleone and Paris's Champs Elysées are home to most of the designer flagship stores.

Growing competition in the retail sector has led to a range of responses, including astronomical investments in store designs that aim to deliver an unforgettable experience. Unsurprisingly, this type of flagship *store* becomes a tourist attraction more than a shopping destination. Those who want to buy a Prada bag want to have a "Prada experience", which involves enjoying the luxury of a visit to a hyper-curated store.

In Italy, AEG and Olivetti pioneered in "identity design": they were the first to design a coherent formal design for their buildings, advertisements, products and points of sale. In these cases, the architecture reflected the brand in terms of the consistency of its design and visual appearance.

In the luxury retail sector, such distinctions are particularly important, as it is both inside and outside of a store that a brand's identity is communicated and experienced.

Examples abound: the most recent being the creative partnership between the historic French fashion house Louis Vuitton (the flagship for luxury giant LVMH) and American architect Peter Marino.

After a year of restyling refurbishments, the Louis Vuitton boutique in London's central New Bond Street reopened its doors in November 2019 under the aegis of fine art. Aiming to replicate the gallery experience, the store houses 43 works by 25 artists, including site specific commissions by Sarah Crowner, Jim Lambie, Josh Sperling, Farhad Moshiri and Matt Gagnon, and works by multi-million dollar artists such as James Turrell, Andreas Gursky, Alex Katz and Tracey Emin, who created a neon sculpture in the heart of the store.

In Seoul that same year, Louis Vuitton opened its monumental store in the Gangnam district, a collaboration between Marino and Frank Gehry, who designed the building's curved glass façade that recalls the Fondation Louis Vuitton in Paris. French fashion house Chanel also entrusted Peter Marino with the design of its first flagship store in Seoul, which opened in March 2019. An art gallery as well as a shop, the space houses 30 works by contemporary artists that the architect selected especially to complement its design. Versace commissioned the Curiosity studio and starchitect Gwenael Nicolas to renovate the Hong Kong store, using the same concept applied in the Beijing and Florence boutiques.

Louis Vuitton flagship store,
Seoul.

Chanel flagship store, Seoul.

Prada Marfa, permanent
installation created by Danish
artists Elmgreen & Dragset,
Texas.

For its flagship store in the Chinese capital, Valentino preferred a direct collaboration between the brand's creative director Pierpaolo Piccioli and award-winning British architect David Chipperfield. The Fendi fashion house entrusted the Milan-based Dimorestudio for its boutiques in Saint Tropez, Monte Carlo and London. The Italian interior design studio has also designed the Dior boutiques in New York's luxury department store Bergdorf Goodman, in Saint Tropez and the Sonia Rykiel boutique in Monte Carlo.

Architect Smiljan Radic was chosen to collaborate with former creative director Sarah Burton at Alexander McQueen's store on Old Bond Street in London, while Bulgari's impressive Fifth Avenue store in New York is once again the work of Peter Marino. The boutiques of Emporio Armani in Las Vegas, Dolce & Gabbana in Soho and Dover Street Market in Manhattan, on the other hand, bear the signature of New York-based Richard H. Lewis Architect. Celine has also focused on art: from 2019, creative director Hedi Slimane has chosen to include paintings, sculptures and installations inside selected boutiques, including those in New York, Tokyo, Paris, London, Milan, Shanghai and Beijing.

Luxury boutiques are increasingly a far cry from the idea of a standard, globalised store. Their success has been defined by three basic elements: distinctive design, a celebrity architect and media engagement. Luxury stores have become an integral part of the urban fabric, attracting visitors as tourist attractions in their own right.

Louis Vuitton flagship store,
London.

Online

The internet has changed the way people shop. E-commerce is the buying and selling of products or services via the internet. Today, e-commerce is a daily activity, the mere thought of living without it seems unfathomable, complicated and inconvenient.

The history of e-commerce begins in 1995 with the invention of Amazon and eBay, and continues to mutate with new technologies, innovations and thousands of companies entering the online market every year. E-commerce and the internet evolve in symbiosis: in 1991, the World Wide Web opens to the public, with Amazon symbolising the success of virtual commerce on a global scale, paving the way for millions of other companies. The convenience, security and user experience of e-commerce has improved exponentially since its timid beginnings. Today, you don't even need a desktop computer anymore: just a mobile device with an app or a browser, thanks to which you can find almost any retail product available on the market, at the best prices, from anywhere and at any time. Brands and retailers no longer even need a traditional store, all to the benefit of efficiency.

No wonder e-commerce is one of the fastest growing industries in the world. In fashion, while traditional brands have been slow to embrace e-commerce and new technologies, some digital native innovators such as Yoox, Net-a-Porter and Asos have changed the rules of the game thanks to novel retail strategies.

In 2000, people only bought clothes they had seen, touched and tried on. In 2020, millions of people around the world chose and bought designer clothes online on Net-a-Porter. The sturdy black box wrapped in a grosgrain ribbon that arrives daily in customers' homes, containing clothes and accessories fresh from the catwalk, has become a symbol of online retail success in the high-end fashion sector.

At Net-a-Porter, wrapped in dozens of layers of the finest black tissue paper, every purchase is treated as though it were a special gift. In 1999, Net-a-Porter founder Natalie Massenet picked up a leaflet in a branch of Barclays Bank, which beared the slogan "Are You an Entrepreneur?". Daughter of an American journalist and a British model, and married to a French investment consultant, thirty-four-year-old designer, *Tatler* fashion writer and former literature student, Ms Massenet had planned to open a chain of coffee shops before launching Net-a-Porter, but her fashion instincts would prove victorious [2].

Her career in the industry began as an editor at *Women's Wear Daily*. Years later, she declared: "I'd just created a magazine for the 21st century... a hybrid between a store and a magazine that was delivered digitally". Now customers are offered the opportunity to buy clothes that have been selected by the expert eye of a fashion editor. As well as offering fashion clothing, editorial content also played a key role in the website's success.

[2] "One-click wonder: the rise of Net-a-porter", *The Guardian*, 10-07-2010.

asos x Klarna.

When buying a luxury product, the transaction itself is only a small part of the experience. The game lies in the ability to offer something above and beyond the product; it is the sale of an experience. From the boxes into which orders are packaged to the brands being sold, the company has built its success on excellence. In 1999, online stores that only sold fashion items operated solely in the discount sector. Net-a-Porter aimed for a completely different approach, becoming a site for the sale of high-end products: the virtual replica of a traditional Chanel or Gucci store, with impeccable service, champagne and an elegant usher.

The year 2000 went down in history as a difficult time for the online industry, due to the dot-com speculative bubble. The internet, which had started to gain popularity in the late 1990s, hit rock bottom that year. The endless optimism for the future of the new medium suddenly turned into mistrust, which in turn led to a serious economic crisis. It seemed illogical to open an online store for luxury goods at a time when investors had lost all hope for the internet, but Natalie Massenet's instincts proved to be right, with her company Net-a-Porter growing to become one of the most popular online destinations for fashion products in the luxury sector. A shining example of modern retail, the Net-a-Porter offices are located on the top floor of London's Westfield shopping centre.

Built on a disused site that was once home to the Franco-British Exposition in 1908, the large shopping centre in White City on the west side of the British capital is a monument to the old "walk-in-and-browse" stores.

In the early 21st century, around the time that Net-a-Porter and other sites like Asos.com emerged, customers weren't interested in buying an item of clothing that they hadn't tried on or touched; purchases were only made on the high street in their city of residence.

In 2000 – the year of the legendary millennium bug – the challenge was to win over brands as well as customers. The very idea of selling through clicks, without a traditional store, was an odd pill to swallow.

Just five years later, brands and designers were clamouring to be considered: Stella McCartney, Yves Saint Laurent, Alexander Wang and RM by Roland Mouret are among those who have even created capsule collections specifically for the site. Being accepted by Net-a-Porter today not only guarantees new customers, but its credibility gives value and visibility to old and new names in fashion.

The majority of the company founded by Natalie Massenet is now owned by Swiss holding company Richemont, and in October 2015 Net-a-Porter merged with Yoox, an Italian company specialising in fashion e-commerce, to form the Yoox Net-a-Porter Group. Since then, Natalie Massenet has moved to the online retail platform Farfetch, as non-executive co-president. The Yoox Net-a-Porter group is now under the leadership of Federico Marchetti, founder of Yoox.

Yoox is the Italian e-commerce company that in 2000 successfully created the virtual fashion store of the same name, along with several other businesses, serving over 100 countries around the world. Yoox.com sells clothing and accessories from multiple brands. Dissatisfied with a traditional career and with a clear vision of the convergence of fashion and the internet, Federico Marchetti, a former financial con-

Vogue and Yoox.com competition sponsors for young designers.

sultant with a degree in economics from Bocconi University in Milan and an MBA from Columbia Business School in the United States, created Yoox in 1999. His goal was not to offer bargain hunting or an outlet site like so many others, his project aimed at a sophisticated group of people who were able to create their own style without having to follow the classic fashion calendar of new collections and discounted goods at the end of the season.

With few connections in the world of fashion or banking, Marchetti left his job at a consulting firm holding a twenty-page business plan and decided to approach venture capitalists, which were relatively rare in Italy at the time. Thanks to support from Elserino Mario Piol, the site was designed and launched within a few months, and would continue to grow over the years.

The company started as a private firm funded by a number of venture capital firms such as Capital Kiwi of Italy, 360 Capital Partner (Net Partners, Italy) and Balderton Capital. In 2009, it became public and was listed on the Milan Stock Exchange. The Yoox Group holds a variety of similar businesses.

These include Yoox online multi-brand shops, which sell at discounted prices, single-brand online shops for established brands and full-price multi-brand online shops. Yoox.com sells luxury brand clothes and accessories at discounted or outlet prices. The company manages this market by purchasing unsold items from past seasons from partner brands and their authorised retailers. This allows brands to sell excess stock without reducing brand value or impacting sales of new stock.

These brands include famous labels such as Dolce & Gabbana, Prada, Gucci, Armani. Some sell only on special occasions, while others create ad hoc limited edition collections. In 2006, Yoox created a separate company, Yoox Services, to manage the online presence of major fashion brands such as Marni, Armani, Diesel, Saint Laurent and Valentino, among others. The company also has its own fashion brand, 8 by Yoox, which was launched in 2018.

In order to fine-tune the collections, Yoox's style team uses advanced, patented artificial intelligence tools to examine trends across social media and online magazines for major markets.

The insights collected in this research phase are crossed with predictive indicators relating to trends, sales data on the site and customer feedback. Starting from this trend table, the creative team scrupulously draws inspiration from the data to produce their collections.

On the opposite side of the fashion spectrum, fast fashion at low prices, ASOS – an acronym for "As Seen On Screen" – was founded in England in 1999. The initial idea was to offer a young clientele inexpensive versions of designer clothes worn by celebrities. Founded by Nick Robertson and Quentin Griffiths, the company became a global company within a few years, and was first listed on the London Stock Exchange in 2001.

Net-a-Porter, presentation.

Today, the website sells over 850 brands including its own range of clothing and accessories, and ships to 196 countries from fulfilment centres in the United Kingdom, the United States and the European Union. Its target group is mainly made up of twenty-somethings looking for novelty at affordable prices.

The own-brand clothing line was founded in 2004, the year in which the company made its first profit of around £120,000. ASOS creations were an instant hit, worn by pop star Rihanna and even Michelle Obama, who casually chose to wear a red and white checked ASOS dress during her husband's election campaign in 2012.

Over the years, the British company has grown overseas, expanding its range to menswear and beauty products as it leads the charge in the online fashion boom.

In 2012 and 2014, two fires that broke out in the Brunswick warehouse destroyed goods worth millions, slowing the British giant's production. Despite this, growth has stead-

Advertising for Yoox Services.

ily continued through innovation, including the use of social networking sites such as Instagram to engage with shoppers, image-driven searches, collections inspired by the brand's own catwalks, and a mix of established international brands and smaller local fashion labels.

From a fashion start-up to a driving internet force with a devoted following, ASOS has been able to face off stiff competition from market newcomers like Boohoo.com and Zalando, as well as retailers investing in and expanding their own online operations.

Just twenty years ago, online shopping seemed like a distant frontier; the idea of a retailer operating exclusively online was almost crazy.

Today, investing online is no longer just an option, even for traditional brands and stores. Omnichannel services are flourishing, causing a shift in mindsets: websites don't simply exist to complement stores, it's stores that support online sales.

The balance of power tends towards digital and the Covid-19 pandemic that broke out in 2020 has specifically accelerated these dynamics. While those who were late on the e-commerce scene are now catching up, those who started

Michelle Obama wears an Asos
dress for her husband's 2012
election campaign.

out on the web are now in a privileged position, despite increasing competition.

THE GLOBAL MARKET

Supply chains

Opposite: Fashion brands land in Beijing.

Overloaded with ethical and environmental issues, fashion has proved to be a fragmented and fickle industry in a process that began with globalisation at the end of the 20th century. The growing demand for low-priced clothing, the pursuit of novelty to stimulate the impulse to buy and increasingly fierce competition in a saturated market have made the fashion supply chain as complex as it is globalised.

Until thirty years ago, the Western world still relied on domestic production and on direct relationships between businesses and suppliers. Today, the industry depends on a workforce situated much further afield, where competitive advantage is measured in terms of speed, quality and efficiency. The variety of products, materials and technologies used in the fashion industry is such that most of the companies involved find themselves operating within a vast network of supply relationships all over the world.

Over the years, however, the level of efficiency in the industry's supply chain has not kept pace with its complexity, and the disconnect between raw material procurement, manufacturers and retailers has generated a number of concerns about the impact of fashion on waste, climate change, low wages and labour exploitation. Clothing production has always been strongly influenced by labour costs, with many brands looking for the cheapest way to do it. Since the 1950s and 1960s, East Asia has been exclusively a low-cost manufacturing area for Western companies. For a long time in the mass market sector, and in textiles-clothing in particular, industrialised countries such as Japan, the United States and Germany have relied on three major Asian producers: South Korea, Taiwan and Hong Kong [1].

[1] Saviolo, Testa, 2005.

As the cost of labour rose in tandem with the development of domestic economies during the 1970s, these countries gradually lost their attractiveness, becoming service centres at the head of new production networks and opening up to emerging areas such as China, Vietnam, the Philippines and Malaysia. Among these, China has risen to world prominence thanks to massive industrial policies that, in the space of a few years, have led it to compete for world leadership in terms of production.

After 1997, coinciding with Hong Kong's return to China, the combined export volume of the two countries reached unprecedented levels, with China becoming the world's largest producer and Hong Kong the financial nerve centre for the entire region. Today, China – the largest beneficiary of the 2005 liberalisation of trade in textiles and clothing – is not only exporting products and activities with greater added value, it has also become a key consumer market itself.

These days, fashion companies face unprecedented challenges due to internationalisation, accelerating trend cycles, consumer demand for quality and transparency, and the need to reduce losses and increase profits in an increasingly competitive market. Driven by the accelerated dynamics created by fast fashion, the unstoppable growth of the fashion industry came to a standstill in 2013 when the clothing industry's most serious fatal accident in modern history occurred in Bangladesh, just outside Dhaka.

On 23rd April, one day before the tragedy, deep cracks appeared in the eight-storey Rana Plaza building. That morning, the workers employed for the production of clothes for major international brands had begged not to be sent

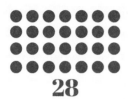

28

brands produced
garments at Rana
Plaza, including Mango,
Primark and Benetton

1133

people lost
their lives

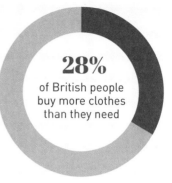

28%

of British people
buy more clothes
than they need

74%

of the survivors
never returned
to work

On 24th April 2013,
all eight floors of the Rana
Plaza garment factory
in Bangladesh collapsed

The British
don't wear
about 17
billion items
they've
bought

8 out of 10

victims were women

inside. The managers did not give in to the protests and, like every other day, more than 2,000 people sat at their respective workstations. Shortly before nine o'clock that morning, the floors began to collapse on top of each other, taking the lives of 1,134 people in less than ninety seconds. The trade unions called it "industrial mass murder". The tragic event suddenly awakened the consciences of the entire industry, shedding light on the industry's more obscure dynamics.

Even customers, who were used to accumulating garments at ridiculously low prices, would now attach importance to the wording on individual labels. Where does the garment come from? Who produced it? Under what conditions? All

of these questions would from now on be at the heart of the modern purchasing decision-making process. Repulsion at what happened at Rana Plaza forced brands and retailers to act.

The word "transparency" became an obligation to be pursued and communicated, on pain of losing customers who were increasingly attentive to details and processes. Ethical as well as environmental reasons lie at the root of the current changes. From H&M to Burberry, documented reports of millions of tonnes of unsold garments burnt or dumped in landfills have made their way around the world. On top of this, fashion has repeatedly been accused of being the most polluting industry in the world, second only to oil. Environmental issues have triggered countless initiatives related to process and product sustainability, and a high awareness of the value and impact of consumer choices.

To this end, technology has offered a lifeline in the thorny world of supply chains. In recent years, the promise of greater efficiency with less waste is becoming a reality,

thanks to a growing number of targeted start-ups. Mobile payment systems, smart fitting rooms and interactive garment search screens are just some of the innovations brands are adopting to speed up the shopping experience and make it easier. However, much more is happening behind the scenes.

The big challenge facing fashion companies is the improvement and digitalisation of the supply chain. Possible scenarios that would require a rapid reaction time include, for example, the need for an increase in the production of a certain product that has been a hit overnight thanks to a social media launch campaign; or there may be a sizing problem in the manufacture of a garment that needs to be reported promptly to the production team, in order to avoid further losses. These emergencies are common to any retail company, and must be handled in a timely manner and with minimal impact, with the help of automated processes. By capturing and analysing data at every stage of the supply chain, fashion companies now have the ability to make more accurate decisions and increase efficiency at all levels.

Social media has also brought about many changes in consumer behaviour and among these is the need for immediacy. Having to adapt to increasingly demanding customers, the need to create products based on data forecasts has also contributed to the adoption of increasingly sophisticated technologies. The same goes for the need – imposed by modern times – to monitor and track the itinerary of each garment, from where raw materials are sourced right up to the finished product, in order to ensure that factory workers are treated fairly. However, the nodal point where the environment and efficiency stand to benefit, is production.

Abandoning old prediction methods tabled on past purchases, trends and intuition, new technologies applied to supply chain management aim to minimise inventory errors through data analysis, so that the right quantity of goods can be produced for a given timeframe during the season. In the future, rather than being destroyed – or even worse, thrown away – it is hoped that the mountains of unsold garments will no longer be a problem for the environment or for company coffers.

Advertising campaign for the H&M
Conscious collection, made with
sustainable materials.

The 9/11 attacks in 2001; the Sars virus of 2002; the controversy in the early 2000s over offshoring services; the global financial crisis of 2008; the trade wars between Donald Trump's United States and Xi Jinping's China and, most recently, the Covid-19 outbreak, have put the long-term viability of a highly decentralised delivery system to the test.

The tendency to produce only what is necessary, according to customers' tastes at any given moment in the shortest possible time, has given way to a "new-old" school of thought in the traditionalist world of fashion. In recent years – also thanks to social media – the need to quickly intercept customer demand, in terms of products, has become the watershed between success and failure. To ensure almost immediate response times, big fashion companies from Zara to Gucci have started using suppliers that are closer to home.

As well as guaranteeing short delivery times for goods by virtue of their proximity to distributors, factories operating in the West aim to ensure and reassure customers of their compliance with high quality standards concerning labour rights.

Nearshoring, automation and sustainability are the three keywords that are driving the evolution of the clothing industry. With the growing importance of online shopping, consumer demands becoming more volatile and difficult to predict, stagnation in key markets, and fiercer competition than ever before, the rules of the system have changed. Mass-market clothing brands and retailers are competing with pure play online start-ups that can replicate popular styles and bring them to customers within a matter of weeks. With the hottest trends now determined by individual influencers and consumers, when it comes to the trends business, the marketing departments of clothing companies have lost much of their clout.

Due to the decline of sales at full price, and growing concerns about the environmental impact of overproduction, the pressure to make a profit means agile production is required, as well as an almost immediate response to consumer demands. The speed of response to market needs and the reorganisation of the range during the season have become crucial. Today's fashion system is profoundly different from that of just a few years ago: reactivity and speed have become essential elements for maintaining competitiveness in a scenario centred on the demands of consumers who are used to creating their own trends.

In addition to concerns about the ecological footprint of offshore procurement, the automation of production processes on several fronts – from prototyping to 3D design – brings production closer to home and reduces labour costs. These processes lead to the acceleration of the entire supply chain and an improvement in terms of sustainability. Using sample tracking or other tools related to measuring product launch campaigns, brands can gauge the popularity of an item by looking at which looks have been most requested by the

press, influencers or stylists, and then predict the demand for each product before launching a collection on the market.

This process allows for more accurate predictions of production needs, reduces potential losses and optimises resources. In the late 20th century, mass-market clothing brands and large chain stores relocated production to Asia in order to benefit from very low labour costs. Today, the cost of labour in countries like China has risen, thereby losing their competitive edge.

General wage increases throughout Asia mean manufacturing in the Far East is no longer as efficient as it used to be. Labour costs in China in 2005 were one tenth of those in the United States; today they are about one third. In some markets close to large consumer countries, the gap between nearshore and offshore labour costs has disappeared: today, for example, Mexico offers lower average productive labour costs than China.

[2] World Trade Organization data, *WT Statistical Review 2019*.

For the Western European market, manufacturing labour costs are still higher than in China, but the gap is narrowing: while hourly manufacturing labour costs in Turkey were more than five times higher than in China in 2005, in 2017 the gap narrowed to 1.6 times [2]. Transport also plays an essential role. From a simple land cost standpoint, nearshoring can be economically viable in many cases, due to the savings in transportation and customs duties costs. From the point of view of logistical costs, it is becoming more attractive for production to get closer to home, but not actually back home. But the real bonus is the shorter delivery times.

By reducing time-to-market, companies can produce more closely in line with demand, reducing excess stock and increasing full-price sell-through. In this model, procurement considerations shift the focus from cost alone to an objective where the net margin on the product in increased, thereby avoiding waste. Despite its attractiveness, the garment making industry in neighbouring countries in the Americas, Turkey, Eastern Europe and North Africa still lags behind Asian manufacturing.

In 2018, the volume of imports from the five largest markets neighbouring the United States did not account for even half of United States imports from China. In these countries, the industry is more fragmented, and the quality and productivity of labour are more unpredictable. Nearshoring also creates a new set of trade-offs and challenges in terms of industry structure, productivity, operating model, sustainability and supply.

The biggest challenge remains the procurement of raw materials, fabrics and components for mass-market clothing production. Only an integrated value chain can deliver the full speed and flexibility promised – without it, longer lead times move higher up in the value chain. Currently, it is in Asia that the main types of fabric are produced and used – China in particular. Mid-range fashion brands have greater supply chain exposure to China than their luxury competitors do.

Although rising labour costs mean that China is no longer as important a producer as it once was, the People's Republic still remains a major source of supply for textiles, while clothing factories have moved to places like Bangladesh and Vietnam.

The countries that benefit most from the nearshoring process are those that have developed and maintained strong skills in the sector – countries such as Turkey, Morocco and Tunisia for denim in Europe [3]. Italy, on the other hand, has lost much of its low- and mid-level production capacity by specialising in production of the highest quality for the luxury market.

[3] McKinsey & Company, "Is Apparel Manufacturing Coming Home?", October 2018.

Over the years, China has become a major consumer as well as a producer. Although multinationals in rich countries could find cheaper production alternatives, many want to keep one foot in China, where they can sell as well as buy.

Furthermore, China has actively encouraged its companies to create supply chains with state assistance through the Belt and Road Initiative, which includes a strong motivation to serve the European market. Analysts say there will always be some life in global supply chains as long as the vast resources of the Chinese state are committed to building infrastructure and establishing trade links with the world.

Vintage and second hand

The popular taste for vintage fashion dates back to the 1990s, but it became a real trend at the beginning of the 21st century. Consumers who choose vintage garments tend to appreciate more original – preferably designer – pieces that are at least 25 years "old", that they can modify and combine with contemporary garments. However, this modern "vintage look" must meet contemporary demands for fit and practicality. Vintage clothing is worn, not simply collected.

Fit, age and originality are the criteria of choice; the result being an eclectic assemblage of garments from different periods.

Onur Bahcivancilar on Unsplash

Bar jacket, Dior, FW 2019.

Due to the investment of money – and time needed for re-search – vintage requires a certain amount of cultural and economic capital. Recent literature points to three main characteristics of vintage style: nostalgia, authenticity and identity [4]. The current popularity of vintage fashion has been linked to a substantial shift in consumer attitudes towards seeking out and using second-hand goods. Consumers and retailers specialising in the genre seem to share a common point of view: it is a reaction against mass-produced fast fashion trends [5]. At the same time, customers who are in-creasingly attentive to detail tend to look for greater indi-viduality in style. The ideal of sustainable fashion has also emerged as a solution to the environmental problems in-herent in the industry's production processes, so the con-cept of sustainability linked to the practice of re-use com-plements the phenomenon of the vintage trend.

Initially marginal, the re-appropriation and re-invention of past styles has become "a highly commodified mainstream phenomenon" [6]. Countless examples illustrate the assim-

[4] Veenstra, A., Kuipers, G., "It Is Not Old-Fashioned, It Is Vintage, Vintage Fashion and The Complexities of 21st Century Consumption Practices", *Sociology Compass*, 7-10-2013.

[5] Cassidy, Bennett, "The Rise of Vintage Fashion and the Vintage Consumer", *Journal of Fashion Practice*, n. 4, 2012.

[6] Palmer, Clark, 2005, p.174.

Left: Saint Laurent bag, Loulou design.
Right: Saint Laurent bag, Betty design.

ilation of vintage into the mainstream fashion industry: reproductions of historical designs like Nike and Adidas Classics, redesigns of iconic pieces from the great couture designers – such as Dior's Bar jacket – or the reinvention of vintage brands, such as Marc Cross.

Reproductions are not the only way this is happening: fashion harks back to bygone days, using names linked to even the personal history of designers of the past. The names Loulou (de la Falaise) and Betty (Catroux) – Yves Saint Laurent muses from the 1970s – are now lent to the brand's most iconic bags. In marketing too, this trend has not gone unnoticed, the revitalisation of old brands is linked to the revival of the feeling of nostalgia. Customers appreciate the products and designs of the past because they are reassuring and recognisable, an antidote to a fast-paced consumer society that is always frantically looking for something new.

The history of vintage clothing as a fashion category is quite recent. During the Victorian era (1837-1901), clothes were considered valuables alongside furniture and silverware as part of the personal estate. Second-hand clothing – an

integral part of the salvaged fabric market – was thriving among the less well-off classes. Towards the end of the 19th century, the germ theory developed by scientists Louis Pasteur and Robert Koch turned the use and sale of second-hand clothes into a morally questionable activity, aimed exclusively at the marginalised and lower strata of society [7].

"Sanitised' by institutions such as the Salvation Army, second-hand clothing goes from suspicious to meaningful, through romantic flea markets and fundraisers for post-war France.

It was the French bohemians in the mid-20th century who elevated the status of second-hand clothes. The unconventional lifestyle of marginalised artists, writers, musicians and actors in major European cities was meant to embody the aspect of "elected poverty" outside the conventional bourgeois fashion of the 1950s. Among the first examples of vintage garments worn to express pride in belonging to a group – and a pinch of glamour – is the raccoon coat.

[7] Le Zotte, J., *From Goodwill to Grunge*, University of North Carolina Press, 2017.

During the 1950s in the United States, a real craze for the old fur coats that were popular in the 1920s breaks out in the Ivy League colleges. Following the stock market crash of 1929, such symbols of wealth, leisure and youthful frivolity quickly lost popularity and clothing shops and department stores were left with stockpiles of them. Before the 1950s, the word "vintage" – a term derived from winemaking – would only have been used to describe luxury cars and fine furniture.

By the middle of the 20th century, cheap raccoon furs have become a symbol of the new democratic ideal of consumer luxury. Leading to a trend of second-hand-as-collector's-item, the raccoon coat craze signifies a move away from middle-class conventions. During the economic boom years, anyone could afford to buy new clothes.

The targeted choice of preferring used clothes testified to the desire to stand out by being "different". In the decades that followed, such brazen vintage and second-hand clothing attracted a variety of consumers, and linked itself to a myriad of political, aesthetic and economic motivations.

In London, from the early 1970s onwards, the vintage and second-hand clothing trade would remain a constant. Shopping guides from the mid-1970s noted numerous specialty retailers, some of which offered in-house tailoring services using salvaged fabrics.

At the time, frequenting such shops was not yet considered a fully acceptable practice and second-hand clothing was mainly worn by the subcultures of the time, in defiance of the mainstream, with the idea of having ownership of previous generations. The duality of subversive practice and economic thrift made vintage a signifier of bohemian morality and aesthetics, particularly in the 1950s and 1960s. The hippy lifestyle was anti-consumerist, a concept that was sartorially translated and communicated through the use of old clothes.

In the 21st century, vintage clothing retains its bohemian roots: the pursuit of individuality and artistic (rather than aristocratic) elitism remain a constant. In Europe and the United States, numerous boutiques specialising in vintage

A The RealReal showroom.

clothing have acquired significant status. Some of these are regularly credited in fashion magazines: shops such as William Vintage, the London emporium founded by William Banks-Blaney in 2010, regularly stock the wardrobes of red carpet movie stars and royalty. The owners of Resurrection and What Goes Around Comes Around in New York and Decades and Lily (Los Angeles) are considered important trendsetters in the industry, having become famous through successful collaborations with the film and TV industry.

Trends aside, ethical and ecological considerations also come into play when it comes to vintage and second-hand clothing in the 21st century. Consumers are increasingly aware of the environmental impact of the fashion industry and are adapting their purchasing habits accordingly. Vintage and second-hand fashion remains an inherently sustainable option.

With reports about the appalling conditions in factories in India and elsewhere, and the waste of natural resources in the production of clothing, people are shopping more consciously and choosing second-hand garments meets these decision criteria. Recent studies suggest that demand is increasing, and this data is supported by the tremendous success of dedicated online platforms.

Since it was founded in 2011 by entrepreneur Julie Wainwright, The RealReal has become a phenomenon: what began as a start-up launched from a home kitchen in San Francisco has transformed the business of authenticated luxury shipping into a dynamic, global movement that promotes not only quality and craftsmanship, but also sustainability and community.

In 2020, The Real Real became a publicly traded company with millions of buyers and sellers worldwide and four retail shops in New York, Los Angeles and San Francisco. The most important European online marketplace for buying and selling authenticated luxury fashion items is Vestiaire Collective, with a team of experts specifically dedicated to checking and authenticating each item sold. Founded in 2009, in the concrete jungle of Paris' 15th *arrondissement*, the company's business has seen phenomenal growth, making multiple millions over the years.

The premise behind Vestiaire Collective is simple: sellers post their designer and non-designer second hand items on the site and anyone can buy them. Once the process is complete, the item is repacked and sent to the customer. When a customer purchases a product, it is sent to one of Vestiaire's authentication hubs for verification by internal experts.

The "direct shipping" option, without authentication, is reserved for selected products, brands and retailers. Vestiaire charges the seller a commission, typically between 20% and 25% of the sale price, and the buyer is charged an authentication fee, up to 2% of the cost of the item.

The business is in a strong position, at the forefront of the thriving resale industry. Vestiaire estimates that the luxury resale market is growing 21 times faster than the traditional luxury sector.

In 2020, the new luxury is to give your wardrobe a second life. For customers looking for unique pieces, however, it is a veritable treasure hunt for instant gratification: the right piece that will help them to differentiate themselves from others; something that will allow them to tell their own story. The use of new terms in the resale market also aims to elevate the status of used clothing and accessories: no

Interior of a Vestiaire Collective store.

longer defined as second-hand, they are pre-loved; loved by someone, treated with care and put back on the market.

These items – often designer pieces – reach prices that are far from affordable. In this case, the function of the resale market is to make up for a shortage of luxury products marketed through traditional channels. One case in point is Hermés handbags: a Kelly or Birkin picked out in the brand's boutiques can take weeks if not months to arrive; a thriving market for authenticated pre-loved pieces in excellent condition has met this growing demand.

Today, we all have powerful computers and smartphones, through which we are always connected to the web. Technology has reduced transaction costs, making resource sharing cheaper and easier than ever, and therefore possible on a much larger scale.

The big change a decade ago was the availability of more data on people and things, which allowed physical resources to be disaggregated and consumed as services. Before the internet, it was possible to rent a surfboard, a power tool or a parking space from someone else, but it was usually more trouble than it was worth.

Established in 2008, Airbnb is the most prominent example of the new "sharing economy", in which people rent beds, houses, flats and other goods directly from each other, all organised over the internet. The sharing economy has been hailed as a new economic system in which under-utilised, privately owned assets such as cars, real estate and clothes are shared for a rental fee through the powerful medium of the internet.

The economic model of the 20th century was based on companies buying raw materials and then producing goods and services which were then sold on the market for a profit. In the 21st century, this is no longer the only way businesses operate. Alongside the market economy, where there are sellers and buyers, owners and workers, producing goods and services and making a profit on the principle of ownership, there is also the sharing economy, where the balance has shifted from ownership to accessibility, from markets to networks, from consumerism to sustainability.

Clothing as a service is a distribution model whereby clothes and accessories are provided to customers on a temporary basis, often through rental or subscription.

Just like streaming movies and music, clothes are now also treated as a subscription service. What at first seemed a curious and relatively cheap idea has over the years legitimately altered the idea of shopping and consumption. Just

Rent the Runway, showroom in New York City.

RTR Unlimited

———

Unlimited rentals.
One monthly price.

One of the Rent the Runway subscription slogans.

a few years later in 2009, Rent the Runway – a New York company that was founded with the initial intention of renting out formal dresses on a short-term basis – conquered the American market.

Today, the company offers monthly subscription packages with unlimited access to designer clothes. The selected garments are delivered directly to your home, fresh from the dry cleaners and with a pre-printed return label, at no extra cost. In addition to its online store, Rent the Runway has five boutiques in the United States, where customers can try on clothes before renting them. The company's success is based on the fact that the customer no longer needs to own a suit in order to be fashionable. The idea has been replicated by Trunk Club, Le Tote and Nuuly in the United States and dozens of others around the world.

Even traditional American retailers have recently joined the rental market: at Bloomingdale's, Ann Taylor, Express, Banana Republic and Levi's you can, for a fee, find clothes to wear and return within the terms of the dedicated service.

Diversity and inclusion

Over the decades, the fashion industry has built its success on ignoring the existence of dark skin, rounded bodies, wrinkles or any feature that is different from the bourgeois, long-limbed, young, white European image. The veneration of whiteness and wealth is not only incidental in the global fashion business, but it has always been central to its vision and embedded into its practices.

From the mid-19th century, the invention of haute couture in Paris established the ideal model of the modern woman: la Parisienne. Across the Channel, her male counterpart was born: the tailored British gentleman. These two sartorial archetypes – the British gentleman and the Parisian woman – only cemented Eurocentric ideologies, patriarchal codes and narratives that portrayed the two main capitals, London and Paris (New York soon joined them), as the pinnacle of civilisation and supreme examples of style [8].

For over a century, fashion dictated its rules; style was determined by Parisian ateliers and followed en masse by a public whose aesthetics were cultivated in the glossy pages of *Vogue* and *Harper's Bazaar*, magazines that were written and edited by mostly white women of bourgeois extraction. Since the 1990s, globalisation has reformulated the cultural context of the fashion system. In the wake of the rapid diffusion of connections across the globe, the myth of Western superiority – in terms of style – has collapsed.

Furthermore, it was the increased popularity of the internet and social media that gave this system based on the West's alleged superiority its final push over the edge. Thanks to social media, everyone from all corners of the globe now has a say. New designers have rediscovered their local traditions without the "exotic" filters imposed by the big European fashion houses, while consumers have raised their voices by showing themselves as they are, diversified by race, age, gender and build. The veil has fallen: the commercial illusion of perfection has crumbled; luxury and elitism have lost their meaning.

Having been accused of racism and of promoting unrealistic ideals and lifestyles, the traditional press – which

[8] Ling, W., Lorusso, M., Segre Reinach, S., "Critical Studies in Global Fashion", *ZoneModa Journal*, 23-12-2019.

was the first to reluctantly give up its sceptre – is now struggling to win back its lost readership.

Over the last five years, scandal in the fashion system has been the order of the day. With almost no representation of racial diversity in the fashion industry – whether on the catwalk, in the atelier or in the boardroom – the race for diversity has been triggered.

Although it was perhaps initially viewed as more of a marketing ploy to please an increasingly sensitive clientele, it is now officially incorporated into business development strategies, from large luxury conglomerates to global media companies. From a glossy magazine, a symbol of the white bourgeoisie and somewhat snobbish, *Vogue* aims to become a diverse and inclusive fashion platform. *Vogue UK*'s September 2020 issue – traditionally the most important one of the year – was entrusted to Misan Harriman, the first black male photographer to shoot a *Vogue UK* cover in its 104-year history.

From advertising to the catwalks, inclusion is on trend: black models are popping up everywhere, including the editorial offices of big fashion companies. The global shift has made fashion more political than it has ever been.

NEW FRONTIERS

Fashion and politics

For decades, corporate neutrality in the fashion industry was the norm – then came the internet and social media, giving the world a voice like never before in history.

In the 21st century, the pace of production and consumption – of products, but also of information – has accelerated and the dynamics of choice and spending have become increasingly complex: a good product is no longer enough to win the favour of consumers. A brand is required to offer more than just quality; values and reputation are equally important attributes.

Fashion is a mirror of the times, it is intrinsically political. Clothing has always been used to express patriotic, nationalistic and propagandistic tendencies, as well as issues relating to class, race, ethnicity, gender and sexuality, but in the last decade the discourse has become even more complex. From the drama of the pandemic, to global warming and issues of gender and race, to the unbearable realisation that fashion's footprint extends from the starry realm of the red carpet to crumbling factories in Bangladesh, 2020 marked a point of no return. Consumers have become increasingly aware, renouncing the old practices of compulsive accumulation, choosing brands and products that align with their values.

As a result of this, civic involvement has turned into corporate values, with designers, companies and retailers launching a series of initiatives, all aimed at harnessing the power of social media – the medium of choice for contemporary fashion.

Either out of moral obligation or because of the opportunities offered by having a stance on social issues to which
their respective customer bases are linked, brands such as
Nike and Gucci have taken the field on sensitive issues.

In February 2018, Gucci decided to support the campaign
for gun restrictions following the shooting at Marjory Stone-
man Douglas High School in Florida, in which seventeen
people lost their lives, reigniting the debate on gun control
in the United States. While large companies rarely take a
position on political issues, preferring to remain neutral,
the Italian mega-brand owned by luxury giant Kering joined
the anti-gun movement March For Our Lives, a student-led
demonstration in support of gun control legislation, which
was also joined by a team representing the company.

Along the same lines, in 2018 Nike chose to include former San Francisco 49ers' quarterback Colin Kaepernick in
its advertising campaign, to celebrate the 30th anniversary
of the "Just Do It" slogan. The former quarterback gained
attention for kneeling during the United States' national anthem before an National Football League game in 2016, as

an act of protest against police killings of African Americans. In retrospect, Nike was right to bet on Colin Kaepernick for his controversial stance: it led to a 31% increase in Nike's online sales. This demonstrates how brands can be more political and have enormous influence (from an ethical point of view), which in turn leads to opportunities to act for positive change.

What Gucci and Nike did was to choose how to take a side. These are very ambitious gestures, but therefore significant: while taking a stand can help brands capture the attention of distracted consumers, doing so on the issues that matter is important in itself. Large global brands like Nike have immense influence on today's society.

While their *raison d'etre* is still commerce, their position within our culture gives them the ability to drive global conversations and the power to influence public opinion in a positive way. Brands are now called on to take full responsibility for the way their businesses operate: promoting people of colour, investing in education, talking about issues, supporting communities, donating and, above all, taking action. A declaration of intent is not a mission; more than ever, words require action and, as a consequence, even fashion brands that have been sitting on the fence for decades now aim to find tangible ways to live up to these values and express them publicly.

Circular fashion

At the Circular Fashion show and talk event in spring 2014 in Stockholm, the concept of "circular fashion" was used by Anna Brismar, founder and owner of Green Strategy, a consultancy firm specialising in circularity and sustainability in the fashion, clothing and textile industry on a global scale. The same year, Swedish fast fashion giant H&M used the term during a public seminar on the industry's environmental impact.

2014 was therefore the year in which the notion of a circular economy entered the political agenda in Europe. The term "circular" has a broader meaning than that of "sustainable fashion", since circular fashion combines the principles of

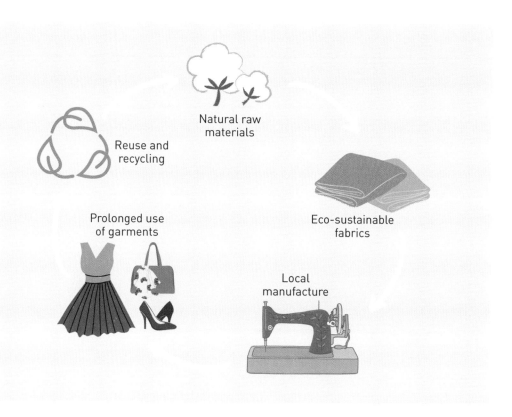

Reuse and recycling

Natural raw materials

Eco-sustainable fabrics

Prolonged use of garments

Local manufacture

sustainability and circularity. It is a revolutionary concept that challenges linear production models based on consumption and waste, focusing on an economic system that minimises waste and makes the best use of resources.

Clothing, shoes and accessories are the centre of attention. The sixteen key principles of circular fashion cover the entire life cycle of a product, from design and sourcing, to manufacturing, transport, storage, marketing and sales, as well as the usage phase and the end of the product's life.

Circular fashion can be defined as clothing, shoes or accessories that are designed, produced, supplied and purchased with the intention of being used and distributed responsibly and effectively in society for as long as possible in their most valuable form, to later be safely returned to the biosphere when no longer required for human use. In other words, fashion products should be designed with high longevity, resource efficiency, non-toxicity, biodegradability, recyclability and good ethics in mind.

Specifically, goods should be produced and purchased with priority given to local resources and efficient and safe practices. Furthermore, they should be used for as long as possible, being cared for, repaired, refurbished and shared among several users over time (through renting/leasing, second-hand usage, exchange etc.). As such, the products should be reimagined to give the materials and components a new lease of life. Finally, the materials and components should be recycled and reused for the manufacture of new products. If unsuitable for recycling, the biological material should instead be composted to become nutrients for plants and other living organisms in the ecosystem. Overall, the life cycle of products should not lead to environmental or socio-economic damage, but should instead contribute to the positive development and well-being of human beings, ecosystems and society in general.

In recent years, the notion of the circular economy has been widely promoted in Europe, North America and Asia. Some key figures and organisations have been particularly successful in promoting the concept and its principles to a wider audience, namely Dame Ellen MacArthur of the Ellen MacArthur Foundation, Walter Stahel, the founding father of performance economics, and Michael Braungart and William McDonough through the Cradle to Cradle Products Innovation Institute.

"The circular economy refers to an industrial economy that is restorative by intention; aims to rely on renewable energy; minimises, tracks and eliminates the use of toxic chemicals; and eliminates waste through careful planning" [1].

[1] Definition by Ellen MacArthur.

Filipe Resmini on Unsplash

In essence, a circular economy means that all materials and products in society are used and circulated among its users for as long as possible, in an environmentally safe, efficient and ethical manner. Waste as we know it does not exist. Instead, waste is seen as a resource or as a "nutrient" for other processes taking place in society. Natural resources, including energy, are used efficiently both during production and for consumption. The use of virgin materials is minimal. Furthermore, priority is given to renewable energy sources and any undesirable environmental impact is prevented or minimised.

All materials used are free of hazardous chemicals and substances, in order to allow a safe and pure stream of raw materials into society. The notion of a circular economy also implies a distinction between biodegradable components, or nutrients, and technically or synthetically manufactured components that cannot decompose naturally. Consequently, in a circular economy, two types of cycles can be distinguished: biological and technical. For the fashion industry, this means that natural fibres such as cotton, silk, wool, viscose and wood are considered natural nutrients and should flow in their own biological cycles, or be separable from any technical components. If left untreated, they can eventually decompose safely in the environment (soil, water, etc.). Conversely, polyester, nylon, acrylic, metals and plastics are considered technical components and must be recycled in separate streams. If recycled optimally, they can be used several times without any loss of quality, remaining useful in a continuous cycle.

Since technical (synthetic) and biological (natural) components must be treated separately, products containing two or more types of materials must be designed to allow easy separation of the individual parts. This makes it easier to repair and replace components, as well as to redesign (upcycle) and ultimately recycle individual material types after use. This concept, called "design for disassembly", is a central principle of the circular economy.

In order to support an integrated circular economy, various infrastructures, modes of collaboration and new business models should be established. Also, new design practices are introduced and new services are provided to customers. The goal is to maximise product longevity and durability through design and procurement specifications, as well as with the support of repair, redesign and recycling services. For a fashion company, this may involve offering customers the option to rent clothes instead of selling them new ones. The company could also provide repair services, whereby customers deliver damaged products for repair or receive a repair kit, so they can mend them at home. Redesign is another service that a company can offer. It can also provide products on demand, which is a bespoke service called "purchasing on-demand". According to the Ellen MacArthur Foundation:

"The circular economy supports the need for a 'functional service model' in which manufacturers or retailers increasingly retain ownership of their products and, where possible, act as service providers who sell the use of products, not their unidirectional consumption. This change has a direct impact on the development of effective and efficient distribution systems and on the dissemination of business models and product design practices that lead to more sustainable products that facilitate disassembly and renewal and possibly take into account product or service layers".

The PLEASEDONTBUY campaign by Twinset, a service for the rental of the brand's clothes.

At present, most fashion products are made from new fabrics, and are sold, worn, discarded and finally sent to landfill or worse – incinerated. In 2019, fashion sales skyrocketed, with 114 billion garments sold globally, or 15 new items per person. Buying fewer items of clothing, and using them several times, helps to slow down the pace and reduces pollution, overproduction and all the problems that go with it.

One of the most iconic brands to wave the sustainability flag is Stella McCartney. The British designer and her eponymous brand immediately embraced the use of innovative materials that have a reduced environmental impact, such as Econyl, a recycled nylon that uses state-of-the-art technology to transform discarded nylon waste into top quality yarn. Econyl can be recycled indefinitely, a feature that makes it perfectly circular. The brand is committed to promoting conservative agricultural practices and designing products that are made to last over time.

A complete reimagination of the fashion industry as we know it, and moving to a new circular economy, will re-

quire exceptional levels of collaboration along the value chain and the implementation of new sustainable business models.

REGENERATIVE AGRICULTURE

The new frontier of sustainable fashion is regenerative agriculture. For organic materials such as cotton, cellulose and wool to meet the standards of the circular economy, they must be grown in a way that conserves the nutrients of the soil in a sustainable way. While environmental discourse often depends on the idea of sustainability – that is, maintaining the current state of the planet and taking care not to degrade it – regenerative agriculture assumes that some things have already been so damaged that they need to be rebuilt, and applies this idea to soil health.

According to the non-profit organisation Regeneration International, the term refers to "farming and grazing practices that reverse climate change by rebuilding soil organic matter and restoring degraded soil biodiversity". Healthy soil is rich in living microorganisms such as fungi, bacteria and protozoa and needs biodiversity to grow healthy plants, sequester carbon from the atmosphere, and absorb water

properly. While intensive agriculture destroys these micro-scopic lifeforms, regenerative agriculture helps to rebuild their ecosystem.

Briefly put, it takes the foundations laid by organic farming and elevates them to the next level by including the agri-cultural practices that benefit the soil, the plants that are being cultivated and the animals that are being raised.

French luxury conglomerate Kering, which owns brands such as Gucci, Saint Laurent, Bottega Veneta and Balen-ciaga, has been on a sustainable mission since April 2012. With a 10-year plan to significantly reduce its carbon foot-print, the company announced a partnership with The Sa-vory Institute (an NGO dedicated to supporting holistic land management and regenerative practices) in 2018, with the aim of supporting verified regenerative sourcing solutions and expanding the framework of regenerative agriculture in global fashion supply chains. Since two-thirds of the en-vironmental impact occurs at the beginning of the supply chain in terms of raw materials, the partnership's goal is to identify and develop a network of farms that Kering can use to produce leather and fibres such as cashmere, wool and cotton.

The practices involved in regenerative agriculture are varied and depend in part on the type of farm in question: they might include the use of natural manure rather than synthetic fertiliser or the abrogation of chemical pesticides. Other practices include crop rotation (growing different types of crops on the same plot in different seasons to optimise nutrients in the soil); intercropping (growing two or more crops in the same space at the same time, such as food crops between rows of cotton); and planting windbreaks (rows of trees on the edge of a field, in order to shelter it from the wind and prevent soil erosion). These natural practices offer numerous benefits, ranging from the prevention of desertification to making plants more resistant to pests and producing more nutritious food crops.

Regenerative agriculture also produces higher quality fibres and leather, which is a clear advantage for manufacturers of clothing and accessories operating in the luxury fashion sector. In addition to carbon sequestration (a natural process in which carbon dioxide is removed from the atmosphere and stored in the soil through a complex mix-

PATAGONIA: "The Greenest Product Is The One That Already Exists"

DON'T BUY THIS JACKET

COMMON THREADS INITIATIVE

REDUCE
WE make useful gear that lasts a long time
YOU don't buy what you don't need

REPAIR
WE help you repair your Patagonia gear
YOU pledge to fix what's broken

REUSE
WE help find a home for Patagonia gear
you no longer need
YOU sell or pass it on*

RECYCLE
WE will take back your Patagonia gear
that is worn out
YOU pledge to keep your stuff out of
the landfill and incinerator

REIMAGINE
TOGETHER we reimagine a world where we take
only what nature can replace

Patagonia, advertising campaign for sustainability.

ture of compounds, consisting of decaying plant and animal tissue, microbes and carbon associated with soil minerals), regeneratively farmed land helps to counteract other side effects of climate change, such as flooding, by making the land better able to absorb water.

Although regenerative agriculture has great potential in terms of environmental benefits, many obstacles remain, chief among them being high conversion costs: for a farm, the transition to regenerative agriculture is a multi-year process that requires considerable investment on the part of the farmers themselves. The regenerative agricultural movement is still in its infancy, and few clothing products are made from regeneratively grown fibres.

Patagonia is among the pioneering brands. The American company has for years been at the forefront of research into sustainable ways to produce its outdoor collections. A promoter of organic cotton farming since the early 1990s, in 2020 the company launched its first collection of T-shirts made from regenerative cotton sourced from farms in India.

Technology in the service of the environment

Over the last twenty years, technology has transformed every aspect of life, and fashion, albeit with difficulty, has kept pace, adapting to a changing world and the demands of increasingly demanding consumers. The fashion industry has long been called into question for its outdated and destructive practices. Today, sustainability and transparency have risen to the top of the agendas of major company CEOs, pushing them to explore alternatives to the same old materials and manufacturing practices that have been used for decades.

NEW MATERIALS

The search for more sustainable raw materials means rediscovering and redesigning forgotten materials, as well as inventing high-tech fibres that are capable of offering high aesthetic and functional standards. In the past, fibre technology and material sciences were limited to specialist use in sports and professional settings, that is, on the fringes of the mainstream fashion industry. Today, this is no longer the case. Many of the major brands have joined the new "materials revolution", characterised by innovation, experimentation, strong investments and a growing commitment to sustainability.

Cutting-edge technologies have transformed fashion companies into multidisciplinary enterprises that are involved in more complex processes than just conventional clothing production and trade. Today's renewed spirit of change is reflected in an updated lexicon of innovative synthetic and natural fibres.

Bio-fabricated leather, biodegradable fabrics, e-textiles and fibres made from unusual products have become key concepts in the future of manufacturing, as well as contributing to new business opportunities. Based on research by strategy consulting firm McKinsey, fashion companies filed eight times more patent applications for innovative fibres in 2019 than in 2013.

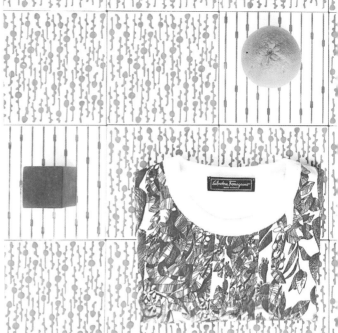

Fibre innovation and the use of sustainable materials represent a new field of development for the fashion industry. Some major areas of innovation are proving particularly promising. So-called "smart" fibres containing chips, for example, are attracting tremendous interest. And then there are yarns made from natural waste raw materials such as Orange Fiber.

In 2013, Adriana Santanocito, then a student in Milan, and her friend and colleague Enrica Arena had the idea of doing something useful with the huge quantities of orange peels left behind by orange squeezing machines. Italy alone produces about 700,000 tonnes of orange waste per year and several companies have been sued over the years for improper disposal of the waste produced by pressing oranges. In collaboration with the Polytechnic University of Milan, the friends developed and patented an innovative process that became a reality thanks to €500,000 in funding from private investors, the European Union and the H&M Foundation. The new fabric made from orange peel is similar to silk, and is now part of Salvatore Ferragamo's accessories collections.

Orange Fiber for Salvatore Ferragamo.

The fashion industry is considered the second most polluting sector in the world, but business models are rapidly changing in terms of production and sourcing of materials. Driven by customers who are more sensitive to environmental issues, major brands are striving for change. From waste milk to pineapple leaves, Orange Fiber is just one of several small companies that are experimenting with reusing and reinventing waste to produce fibres for clothing and accessories.

Fili Pari is another Italian start-up that develops and promotes unconventional materials for the textile sector. Founders Alice Zantedeschi and Francesca Pievani have patented Marm More, a microfilm containing real marble dust. Fili Pari's philosophy embraces the values of the circular economy by using marble dust derived from by-products of the stone industry. Once selected and prepared, waste is reused, with the aim of designing new materials that combine style, innovation and technical performance.

In 2018, German company QMilk presented its fibre made from waste cow's milk on the catwalk during the Mercedes-Benz Fashion Week in Berlin, as part of an accessories collection by outdoor clothing brand Vaude. As shiny as silk, the fabric made from milk protein has antibacterial properties, is thermo-regulating, lightweight, absorbent, compostable and flame resistant.

In addition to consumers increasingly orienting their choices towards sustainable products, government policies are moving towards compliance with high standards: the European Union's circular economy package introduces ambitious targets for the recycling of waste, including textiles. The European Union also funds research.

According to a study by the Ellen MacArthur Foundation – the charity that promotes sustainability in the industry – the equivalent of a rubbish truck full of textiles is thrown away every second, while less than 1% of clothes are recycled to make new clothes. Clothing releases half a million tonnes of microfibres into the ocean every year. Furthermore, if nothing is done to change this, the fashion industry will consume a quarter of the world's annual carbon budget by 2050. To date, most of the fashion industry has been based on the use of synthetics – that is, petrochemicals – or on a

Opposite: Fili Pari, production phases.

monopoly of genetically modified cotton. Both are extremely destructive to the environment.

TRACEABILITY AND TRANSPARENCY

Over the last decade, increasingly pressing ethical and environmental issues have eroded consumer confidence in fashion brands. Thanks to the internet, the previously concealed mysteries along the complex supply chains of the fashion system have been revealed, leaving consumers sceptical and wary of established practices that aim to exploit in the name of pure profit.

Now more than ever, consumers expect full transparency along the entire value chain, demanding to know more about a range of issues: where items come from and how they are made, the origin of the design and raw materials, respect for the workforce, and the environmental impact of the production process.

This increased demand for information has made "radical transparency" a trend that the fashion industry has hastened to follow, on pain of losing valuable customers and declining sales. For many years, various fashion brands, from luxury to low cost, have benefited enormously from the manufacturing capabilities of developing countries, while offering little in the way of labour protections.

Skilled artisans with no social or health benefits would sew thousands of garments in dilapidated factories for a few dollars a day, completing orders on behalf of the major international designers. It's not just about fast fashion (companies whose business model is based on producing fashionable clothing as cheaply as possible and whose supply chain issues came to the fore in 2013, following the Rana Plaza tragedy). Even expensive, glitzy catwalk brands indirectly employ thousands of workers in developing countries.

In Mumbai, India, dozens of workshops and export companies act as intermediaries between haute couture brands and highly-skilled artisans, providing design, sampling and manufacturing services. More often than not, customers who are prepared to pay thousands of euros for a designer

garment are unaware of this. In a landscape of increasing consumer scrutiny, the parameters in which fashion brands are judged include creative integrity, sustainable supply chains, value for money, treatment of workers, data protection and authenticity.

Further up the supply chain, transparency has become a central issue. In the purchasing decision process, issues such as fair labour conditions, sustainable resources and respect for the environment are just as important as design and quality, bonuses for which most consumers (66% according to a 2019 McKinsey survey) are willing to pay a premium.

Hoping to regain the trust of disillusioned customers and to avoid front-page scandals, many brands have moved towards radical transparency in their manufacturing process, investing money to address any grey areas and to highlight their best practices in order to create a competitive advantage.

Since 2015, the not-for-profit organisation Fashion Revolution has published an annual transparency index of the major fashion brands, ranking them according to the amount of information they disclose on policies, processes and social and environmental effects, in the context of their operations and supply chains. The index is a tool that incentivises major brands to be more transparent, by encouraging them to disclose more information.

The transparency index is not about which brand does best, but about who reveals the most information. In 2020, the H&M group, C&A, Adidas / Reebok, Esprit, Marks & Spencer and Patagonia were ranked among the most transparent fashion brands in the world. Also in the top 10 are Puma, Asos, Nike and VF Corporation – the company behind brands like The North Face, Timberland and Vans. Those who did not disclose any information included Bally, Jessica Simpson, Max Mara, Mexx and Pepe Jeans, with Tom Ford at the bottom of the list.

Given its particular reliance on complex supply chains, transparency is the key to creating a cleaner and more ethical fashion industry. One of the solutions to this problem has been offered by new technologies such as blockchain, where the entire transaction history can be seen in each network node, so that transparency is increased along the entire supply chain, from sourcing raw materials to the shop.

Blockchain is a term often associated with cryptocurrencies such as bitcoin, but it can have many other applications as well. The potential to transform business operating models remains the most interesting for fashion. In essence, the blockchain decentralises transactions by eliminating the middleman and replacing them with a secure digital record. According to Merriam Webster's dictionary, a blockchain is "a digital database containing information that can be simultaneously used and shared within a large, decentralised, publicly accessible network".

Blockchain technology does not exist in physical form and is therefore somewhat difficult to fully understand. Its potential applications are revolutionary in countless sectors: in the short term, blockchain has emerged as a powerful tool to make the fashion industry more transparent, minimising greenwashing and making consumers more aware of the

Visualsofdana on Unsplash

path their clothes have taken to reach them. When it comes to monitoring the production chain for sustainability, quality or even authenticity, the blockchain becomes tangible as an identification number on each product – something akin to a passport – where all the information on its journey is open, shared and incorruptible.

For example, when a batch of alpaca wool leaves the farm, it is monitored through closed analogue systems or even pen and paper. Usually, a sales invoice and a bill of lading are issued: these provide information on the specific batch and are kept by all parties concerned. When the courier delivers the wool to the textile company, they sign a document and issue a purchase invoice, and so on. These processes accompany the raw material at each stage of the chain, until it is transformed into the final product. By storing all this information in a blockchain system, rather than in internal or analogue systems, blocks of information can be accumulated and used to validate the product. Once the information has been recorded, it remains accessible forever to anyone with a QR code or NFC reader on their mobile phone. Each piece is therefore provided with a unique code which, when read, displays its entire history in detail.

This information system is still in the experimental stage and requires shared participation throughout the supply chain. Many issues remain unresolved, but in recent years several start-ups have been working on the implementation of this revolutionary technology, which is already being used successfully, albeit on a small scale, for example in the food sector.

Fashion after the crisis

Clothes reveal the values and aspirations of the wearer, a statement that is all the more valid in times of unrest and upheaval. 2020 was one of the most difficult years in living memory and fashion, as a powerful visual indicator of the times, reflected its values, hopes and fears.

At intervals throughout history, the world and the societies that populate it have gone through catastrophic events that have altered their course, with significant repercussions affecting everyday practices, including clothing. In the last century, for example, the two world wars led to a series of restrictive measures on the use of raw materials that were needed for making clothes, but fashion did not stop when war was declared.

The first Parisian clothing collections that were presented after the start of the World War II were practical without forsaking aesthetics. Coats, suits, trousers, zip-front jumpsuits and printed cotton dresses were designed with a distinctive sense of style.

Between bombings and austerity, life went on and women and men still cared about their appearance. Hope endured and so did fashion. "Make do and mend" was the motto for all countries involved in the World War II. Restrictions on

fabric, leather and metal required clever solutions to make the best use of what was available. In order to save on labour and materials, as well as to minimise production costs, single-breasted suits replaced double-breasted, trousers no longer had turn-ups, the number of pockets was limited and both zips and elastic waistbands were banned, except for women's underwear.

Similar trends ran throughout the 1930s' Great Depression: Americans turned their backs on the festive mood of the Roaring Twenties, evening-to-morning flapper dresses ended up locked in drawers in favour of more reserved styles. However, fashion not only survived, but experienced a period of extraordinary creativity.

The years leading up to the World War II were among the most complex in terms of trends. On the one hand, fashion was influenced by the economic depression that hit the entire Western world for the whole decade; on the other hand, fashions of the 1930s were characterised by extreme elegance, with trends largely determined by the taste of high society, of film stars and celebrities whose legends were being cemented in the collective consciousness at that time. In a peculiar way, these two influences managed to coexist, creating simple yet sophisticated styles.

What better example than that of Elsa Schiaparelli's immense creativity. In 1937, she showcased her champagne-coloured silk dress painted with red lobsters (signed by none other than artist Salvador Dalí, a personal friend of the Roman designer). The elegant dress won over Wallis Simpson, who chose it for Cecil Beaton's *Vogue* photo shoot, shortly before her marriage to Edward VIII.

Affordable fabrics, catalogue clothing at reasonable prices, and homely ingenuity allowed anyone to copy the styles of glamorous Hollywood stars and high society ladies. Then came the war to shake things up, but in the 1950s, as the world came out of the war in tatters, a new silhouette emerged, embodied by Christian Dior's New Look: fitted jackets, padded hips, slim waists and A-line skirts represented a return to femininity, the joy of dressing up and a new image of prosperity.

In general, it can be said that clean lines characterise design when times are tough; few designers embrace extravagance when the going gets tough. In the 1970s and late 1990s, recessions again showed their effects. The oil crisis put paid to the futuristic experiments of the 1960s, while in the late 1980s, spandex jumpsuits, heavy bijoux and reinforced shoulder pads gave way to softened silhouettes and lots of nostalgia. In times of uncertainty, simplicity becomes the watchword.

In a 1974 essay entitled *Recession Dressing*, in response to the economic recession that had begun a year earlier, fashion expert Kennedy Fraser wrote: "The old interest in the cautious principle of spending more on fewer clothes of better quality is back". "Less is More", the most popular maxim of the legendary architect-designer Mies van der Rohe, was put into practice in 1990s fashion. Calvin Klein is perhaps the most popular example; at that time, a waif-like Kate Moss was his muse. Miuccia Prada indulged in minimalism in 1998 with an austere collection characterised by simple lines, black and white and no accessories [2].

[2] Caielli, I., "La moda in tempi di crisi", *vanityfair.it*, May 2020.

Above: Elsa Schiaparelli, 1937.
Right: Elsa Schiaparelli, SS 2017.

The year 2020 – the *annus horribilis* of the Covid-19 pandemic – ravaged the world, claiming hundreds of thousands of lives and burning billions in GDP, with record-breaking figures that evoke the black swan theory: an unexpected event from devastating consequences. Fashion has seen its importance redefined and many have even questioned its relevance: in the midst of a pandemic, uprisings for social justice and a looming climate crisis, what's the point of new clothes?

The closure of shops and factories, a drop in consumption rates and the reputational damage caused by a production system that is too often anchored in abysmal inequalities, have all undermined the foundations of the fashion world, which was already in crisis well before 2020 arrived on the calendar.

When navigating an uncertain future, you don't dress to attract attention. During lockdown, people's priorities shifted to maximum comfort and a renewed interest in clothes that are loved, already worn, cosy; the antithesis of fast fashion. Meanwhile, the need for social distancing found a new ally: digitisation. Thanks to virtual participation, online fashion weeks welcomed a wider audience.

In January 2021, Prada released its first campaign under the creative co-direction of Raf Simons and Miuccia Prada. Well accustomed with the intellectual side of fashion, the Milanese brand has grasped the new sentiment, in an industry that is still grappling with the imperative of rad-

ical change. The campaign poses a series of meaningful questions: is the new still relevant?, should we slow down or speed up?, is creativity a gift or a skill?

The questions are posed in the form of a dialogue: when visiting the Prada website, users are invited to interact, with the possibility of answering and asking new questions. In the press release, Prada stated that the campaign was created to investigate relevant issues facing our society today: "The questions themselves meditate on important topics: self-perception, views on technology, ideas about humanity – diversity, inclusivity, sustainability". But the change went deeper still. The ideals of exponential growth, personal success, instant gratification, and the expression of identity through consumption – exalted in the 1980s and 1990s – turned out to be unrealistic, as well as destructive, fantasies.

After decades of unbridled consumption, the pandemic caused by Covid-19 has realigned individual priorities on a more intimate scale. The need for affection, the redis-

SHOULD WE

SLOW DOWN

OR

SPEED UP?

ANSWER

AT

PRADA

.COM

covery of domesticity, of do-it-yourself and repair, and the
renunciation – albeit forced – of consumption at all costs,
have also led to a rethink of fashion: out with disposable
fast fashion, in with conscious shopping, or buying less but
better, with a greater propensity to invest in higher quality items at a higher price. When incomes are in free fall,
spending more on a single garment seems counterintuitive,
but less disposable income means less money to waste on
clothing each season, so better quality and designs that are
made to last are prioritised.

In this context, the novelty of fashion trends' rapid turnover (which, for decades, was the industry's most powerful
driving force) has been challenged. At the same time, and
in the same spirit, resale and second-hand marketplaces
have gained ground, enjoying great market success and unprecedented interest from investors. In March 2021, Henry
Pinault, the tycoon at the head of "traditional" luxury empire Kering, acquired 5% of Vestiaire Collective, the most
important resale platform in Europe.

HOW IS

ANSWER

UNIQUE

AT

DIFFERENT

FROM NEW?

PRADA

.COM

Fashion will always play a key role in society, both from a functional and a cultural point of view. On an individual level, fashion gives people the power to express themselves; on a collective level, fashion allows people to connect with others and gives them a sense of belonging. Future challenges will require the industry to live up to its responsibilities to participate in the creation of a more positive, collective future.

BIBLIOGRAPHY

Adams, W. H., *On Luxury*, Potomac Books, Dulles, 2012.

Agins, T., *The End of Fashion*, Harper, New York, 1999.

Baldini, C., *Sociologia della moda*, Armando Editore, Rome, 2008.

Barthes, R., *Lessons on the Philosophy of Fashion. Forme e significati dell'abbigliamento*, Einaudi, Turin, 2006.

Barthes, R., *The Fashion System,* University of California Press, Berkeley, 1990.

Benjamin, W., *Parigi, capitale del XIX secolo*, Einaudi, Turin, 1986. [English Translation: "Paris: Capital of the Nineteenth Century", *Perspecta*, vol. 12, MIT Press, 1969.]

Berry, C. J., *The Idea of Luxury: A Conceptual and Historical Investigation*, Cambridge University Press, 1994.

Breward, C., *The Culture of Fashion: A New History of Fashionable Dress*, Manchester University Press, Manchester, 1995.

Breward, C., *Fashion*, Univesity Press Oxford, Oxford, 2003.

Breward, C., Gilbert D., *Fashion's World Cities*, Berg, New York, 2006.

Byrne Paquet, L., *The Urge to Splurge: a Social History of Shopping,* ECW Press, Toronto, 2003.

Cappellari, R., *Marketing della moda e dei prodotti di lifestyle*, Carocci, Rome, 2016.

Celefato, P., *Lusso*, Meltemi, Rome, 2003.

Church Gibson, P., *Fashion and Celebrity Culture*, Bloomsbury, London, 2012.

Codeluppi, V., *Che cos'è la moda*, Carocci, Rome, 2002.

Coleridge, N., *The Fashion Conspiracy*, Octopus Publishing, London, 1988.

Corbellini, E., Saviolo, S., *L'esperienza del lusso. Mondi, mercati, marchi*, Rizzoli Etas, Milan, 2007.

Corner, F., *Why Fashion Matters*, Thames & Hudson, London, 2014.

Crane, D., *Fashion Questions. Classe, genere e identità nell'abbigliamento*, Franco Angeli, Milan, 2004.

Currid-Halkett, E., *The Sum of Small Things: A Theory of the Aspirational Class*, Princeton University Press, 2017.

Díaz-Bustamante, M., García, S., Puelles, M., *Image of Luxury Brands: A Question of Style and Personality*, SAGE Open, vol. 6, 2016.

Dorfles, G., *La (nuova) moda della moda*, Costa & Nolan, Genoa, 2008.

Drake, A., *The Beautiful Fall. Fashion, Genius and Glorious Excess in 1970s Paris*, Bloomsbury, London, 2006.

Eco, U., *Storia della bellezza*, Bompiani, Milan, 2004.

Fabris, G., Minestroni, L., *Valore e valori della marca*, Franco Angeli, Milan, 2004.

Fabris, G., *Il nuovo consumatore: verso il postmoderno*, Franco Angeli, Milan, 2003.

Featherstone, M., *Consumer Culture and Postmodernism*, Sage Publications Ltd, London, 1991.

Flügel, J. C., *Psicologia dell'abbigliamento*, Franco Angeli, Milan, 2003.

Frisa, M. L., *Le forme della moda. Cultura, industria, mercato: dal sarto al direttore creativo*, Il Mulino, Bologna, 2015.

Gilovich, T., Keltner, D., Nisbett, R. E., *Social Psychology*, W.W. Norton & Company, United States, 2011.

Gladwell, M., *The Tipping Point, How Little Things Can Make a Big Difference*, Back Bay Books, United States, 2002.

Gnoli, S., *Un secolo di moda in italiana. 1900-2000*, Meltemi, Rome, 2005.

Grant, L., *The Thoughtful Dresser*, Scribner, New York, 2009.

Hegermann-Lindencrone, L. de, *In the Courts of Memory*, Harper & Brothers, New York, 2015.

Hunderhill, P., *Why We Buy. The Science of Shopping*, Simon & Schuster, New York, 1999.

Kapferer, J. N., *The New Strategic Brand Management: Creating and Sustaining Brand Equity*, Kogan Page, London, 2004.

Katz, E., Lazarsfeld, P., *Personal Influence*, Routlege, United Kingdom, 2017.

Kawamura, Y., *Fashion-ology*, Bloomsbury, London, 2005.

Kilbourne, J., *Can't Buy My Love. How Advertising Changes the Way We Think and Feel*, Touchstone, New York, 2000.

Klapp, O., *Collective Search for Identity*, Holt, Rinehart & Winston, Vancouver, 1969.

Klein, N., *No Logo. Economia globale nuova contestazione*, Baldini & Castoldi, Milan, 2001.

Kotler, P., Keller, K. L., *Maketing Management*, Pearson Education Incorporate, London, 2015.

Kotler, P., Kartajaya, H., Setiawan, I., *Marketing 4.0. Moving from Traditional to Digital*, John Wiley & Sons, Hoboken, 2017.

Laver, J., *Costume and Fashion: A Concise History*, Thames & Hudson, London, 2002.

Lipovetsky, G., *L'impero dell'effimero. La moda nelle società moderne*, Garzanti, Milan, 2007. [Englist Translation: *The Empire of Fashion: Dressing Modern Democracy*, Princeton University Press, 1994.]

Lurie, A., *The Language of Clothes,* Vintage Books, Univiversity of Michigan, 1981.

McDowell, C., *La moda oggi*, Phaidon, London, 2009.

Moore, K., Reid, S., *The Birth of Brand: 4000 Years of Branding History*, Munich, 2008.

Morini, E., *Storia della moda, XVIII-XX secolo*, Skira, Milan, 2000.

Morris, D., *Manwatching: Field Guide to Human Behavior*, Harry N Abrams Inc, United States, 1977.

Muzzarelli, M. G., *Breve storia della moda in Italia*, Il Mulino, Bologna, 2011.

Muzzarelli, M. G., Riello, G., Tosi Brandi, E. (eds), *Fashion. Storia e storie*, Bruno Mondadori, Milan, 1988.

Nietzsche, F., *Umano, troppo umano*, Mondadori, Milan, 1970. [English Translation: *Human, All Too Human*, Barnes & Noble, 2018.]

Okonkwo, U., *Luxury Fashion Branding: Trends, Tactics, Techniques*, Palgrave Macmillan, 2007.

Packard, V., *The Status Seekers*, David McKay, New York, 1959.

Palmer, A., Clark, H., *Old Clothes, New Looks: Second-Hand Fashion*, Berg Publishers, 2005.

Perniola, M., *Il sex appeal dell'inorganico*, Einaudi, Turin, 2004.

Perrot, P., *Fashioning the Bourgeoisie: A History of Clothing in the Nineteenth Century*, Princeton University Press, Princeton, 1994.

Pine, B. J., Gilmore, J., *The Experience Economy*, Harvard Business School Press, Boston, 1999.

Pine, B. J., Gilmore, J. H., *Authenticity. What Consumers Really Want*, Franco Angeli, Milan, 2009.

Pizza, P., *Psicologia sociale dell'abbiglamento*, QuiEdit, Verona, 2010.

Polhemus, T., *Trickle Down, Bubble Up*, in The Fashion Reader, Berg, Oxford, 2007.

Polhemus, T., Procter, L., *Fashion & Anti-Fashion. An Anthropology of Clothing and Adornment*, Thames & Hudson, London, 2011.

Riello, G., *La Moda: Una storia dal Medioevo a oggi*, Laterza, Rome-Bari, 2012.

Riello, G., McNeil, P., *Luxury: A Rich History*, Oxford University Press, Oxford, 2016.

Rizzi, B., Milani, S., *Visual merchandising e visual marketing*, Franco Angeli, Milan, 2013.

Saviolo, S., Testa, S., *Le imprese del sistema moda. Il management al servizio della creatività*, Etas, Milan, 2005.

Segre Reinach, S., *Manuale di comunicazione, sociologia e cultura della moda, 4. Orientalismi*, Meltemi, Rome, 2006.

Segre Reinach, S., *La moda. Un'introduzione*, Laterza, Rome-Bari, 2010.

Segre Reinach, S., *Un mondo di mode. Il vestire globalizzato*, Laterza, Rome-Bari, 2011.

Semprini, A., *La marca*, Lupetti, Milan, 2003.

Silverstein, M. J., Fiske, N., *Trading Up. La rivoluzione del lusso accessibile*, Etas, Milan, 2004.

Simmel, G., *Philosophie der Mode*, Suhrkamp, Frankfurt, 1995.

Steele, V., *Paris Fashion*, Oxford University Press, London, 1998.

Steele, V., *Encyclopedia of Clothing and Fashion*, vol. 1-3, Charles Scribners Sons, New York, 2004.

Tungate, M., *Fashion Brands. Branding style from Armani to Zara*, Kogan Page, London, 2005.

Veblen, T., "La teoria della classe agiata. Studio economico sulle istituzioni", Il Saggiatore, Milan, 1969.

Vejlgaars, H., *Anatomy of a Trend*, McGraw-Hill Education, New York, 2007.

Wilson, E., *Adorned in Dreams: Fashion and Modernity*, Virago, London, 1985.